50 Days to Your Mental Jubilee

Michelle Trotter

Copyright © 2019 Michelle Trotter
Scriptures used by the permission of Zondervan.
All rights reserved.
ISBN: 9781079515626

Acknowledgements

I would first like to give all Glory and Honor to my Lord and Savior, Jesus Christ. He has truly brought revelation, healing, and deliverance to my soul. I have taken Romans 12:2, and through His Word, I have become actively involved in renewing my mind and restoring my life.

I would also like to give honor to my husband, Apostle Willie Trotter, who is perhaps my biggest cheerleader and pusher. Without his hand in my back, I'd probably still be a bench warmer, working behind the scenes. I thank my children De'Jeanne, Ashley, and Adam, and my grandchildren Marshae, Braylen, and Judah, for unselfishly sharing me for the sake of this Kingdom Assignment.

I also want to acknowledge my family, church family (House of Jubilee Ministries), and friends, who have stood behind me, prayed for me, and encouraged me during this process. Sondra Clarke, my editor, for her expertise and time. Tatiana Wells and Sharonna Miles, for all the assistance and time they took to get me all the way together! To Lisa Turner and Crystal Allen, who were my sounding boards on our 'sister trips.' It is because of you all that I pressed past my own doubts, fears, and inhibitions to pursue the freedom that I experience today. I love you all so much! Your handprints are forever in my back.

And last, but certainly not least, I want to give honor to my Pastor, the late Bishop Charles O. Clarke, Sr., who laid a foundation of faith in my life that is unshakeable. He taught me to love Christ and His Word with everything that is in me. He was (and still is) a constant source of encouragement and inspiration in my life. I love you Dad; I hope I've made you proud.

Table of Contents

Acknowledgements

Foreword

Introduction 1

Day

1	Think About What You're Thinking About!	6
2	Be Always Ready!	9
3	It's A Heart Thing!	12
4	The 'YOU' View	15
5	Watch Your Mouth!	19
6	What Are You Talking About?	23
7	Enlarge Your Borders!	27
8	Becoming a Gardener for Your Soul	31
9	Does Your Life Prove the Will of God?	34
10	Take a Praise Break	37
11	Grace: God's Empowerment!	40
12	God's Abounding Grace	44
13	Grace: God's Divine Power	48
14	A Superior Reality	52
15	Exchanging Realities	55
16	The Mind of Christ	59

17	The Carnal Mind	62
18	The Effects of Carnality on our Reasoning	65
19	Carnal Thinking Leads to Carnal Living	69
20	Take a Praise Break	73
21	You've Been Translated from One Kingdom to Another	76
22	Transitioning Into the New You	80
23	Discovering the New You	84
24	Practice the New You	88
25	Be Careful HOW You Hear	91
26	Let Not Your Heart Be Troubled	94
27	You Get to Choose	97
28	Your Life is in Your Mouth	101
29	The Way That Seems Right, Might Not Be	104
30	Take a Praise Break	108
31	Get Rid of All Anxiety	112
32	Prayer Defeats Anxiety!	115
33	Make Supplication to the Lord	118
34	Come Boldly to God	122
35	Develop a Heart of Thanksgiving	126
36	Receive the Peace of God!	130
37	God Tells Us How to Think	133

38	Fix Your Mind	137
39	God Says, 'Don't Worry'	141
40	Take a Praise Break	145
41	Great Minds Don't Think Alike!	148
42	#TeamMe!	151
43	We Have the Power to Transform!	154
44	An Excellent Soul, Wow!	158
45	We Have the Power for Moral Excellence!	162
46	We Have Strength (Dunamis Power) for All Things!	166
47	We Have Joint Seating With Christ	170
48	Just How High Are We Seated?	174
49	A Renewed Mind	178
50	Take a Praise Break	182
	Appendix	186

Foreword

The *50 Days to Your Mental Jubilee* devotional is a strategy--not just a statement. I believe it captures the very mindset of the heart of God. When God says in Roman 12:2, "be not conformed but be transformed," it is stating exactly what every born again believer must do. I believe this book is a 21st century, cutting edge, must read.

As I think back to the early part of Apostle Michelle's and my life together, I remember her as a very timid, insecure person. But God had a call and a plan for her. I have watched her use the principles in this book and allow them to transform her mind. She began to manage her thoughts and refuse to accept what the devil was trying to create. This ultimately changed her destiny. I believe that she is an Apostle, sent by God, to deliver His people from the prison of their own minds.

When you are born into the Kingdom of God, your spirit is brand new, but your mind has to be renewed. Many born again believers have not experienced freedom nor have they accomplished God-given purpose and goals because of an unrenewed, diabolical mindset. This mindset enslaves them to the tactics, wiles, and schemes of the enemy. Because of this, Satan has kept them locked behind bars of wrong thoughts, fear, anger, rejection, and timidity. Many others struggle with a victim mentality. They constantly feel they are being treated unfairly. They put undue pressure on every relationship to try to be accepted. You may hear them make statements like, "I'm not stupid" or "you think I'm dumb." When we have a negative self-image based on the lies of the devil, we place ourselves in a position where Satan can take us captive at his will. You may have been a part of a family gathering or great event that was torn to pieces in a matter of minutes because of one small misunderstanding. When a person feels rejected and has a low self-image, there is nothing anyone can do to make them feel accepted. This is a work that only God can do. Recognizing the need for a renewed mind is *paramount*. The principles in this book will help to navigate through the confused thoughts and negative paradigms of the mind.

This book is not just a good read but a *handbook* for Kingdom transformation. I believe as you get started on your 50-day journey, you will begin to experience the liberty that results from your mental jubilee. You will go from depression to rejoicing; from fear to faith; and from timidity to boldness. Those who once merely existed will begin to live and thrive. You will emerge from your cocoon, rise up, and fly high as a beautiful butterfly! Don't delay; invest in yourself. Free your mind and your life will follow! God bless you as you start your journey.

Apostle Will Trotter
House of Jubilee Ministries
Cleveland, Ohio

Romans 12:2 MSG

"So here's what I want you to do, God helping you: Take your everyday, ordinary life—your sleeping, eating, going-to-work, and walking-around life—and place it before God as an offering. Embracing what God does for you is the best thing you can do for him. Don't become so well-adjusted to your culture that you fit into it without even thinking. Instead, fix your attention on God. You'll be changed from the inside out. Readily recognize what he wants from you, and quickly respond to it. Unlike the culture around you, always dragging you down to its level of immaturity, God brings the best out of you, develops well-formed maturity in you."

Introduction

You may have heard the old saying 'the mind is a terrible thing to waste.' This is probably one of the most truthful statements ever uttered. The mind is the control center of our entire existence. Without it we can do nothing. If left to itself, the mind could potentially destroy us. Like a garden left to itself, weeds of toxic thoughts will grow and snuff out every good intention and goal. However, if it is tended to, that precious garden has an unlimited potential for greatness!

Years ago, when my son was in high school, I was waiting outside the school for him to come out of basketball practice. It was a rainy evening, and my windshield wipers were on as I waited. I watched the wipers go back and forth, back and forth. As the wipers did their job, I watched as one single stream of rain water would run down the windshield after each wipe. The wiper would wipe, and that one stream of water would reappear and make its way down the window once again. At the top of the windshield, there were probably thousands of new raindrops falling, but as the wiper wiped the viewing area of the windshield, there was only one stream that all the raindrops would have to get to in order to slide down the window.

That day the Lord said to me, "This is what your mind is like." He said, "Imagine that one stream is your stream of thought. It represents your mindset and how your thoughts are processed." That one statement from God changed my life and sent me on a venture. I discovered how important it was that the one 'stream' be pure, purged, and managed properly. All new thoughts, ideas, visions, goals represented by the thousands of raindrops that rested at the top of that windshield had to make their way down that one single stream of a 'mindset.' It became imperative that I make sure my mindset could hold and cultivate all the things that God would say to me, reveal to me, and expect me to carry out in my earthly assignment.

Romans 12:2 says, "And be not conformed to this world: but be ye transformed by the renewing of your mind, that ye may prove what is that good, and acceptable, and perfect, will of God." The Amplified Classic Bible puts it this way: "Be transformed (changed) by the *entire* renewal of your mind." This scripture let me know that God expects His people to renew their minds through His Word. There is a way that we can change any 'stream' of thought, or paradigm, that is not conducive to producing the will of God. It also revealed to me that we have the *ability* to change the way we think and perceive things. We were *designed* by God to be able to change our minds. Glory to God; that is awesome! We need to change our minds because some of the ideas, thoughts, and imaginations we have are twisted and were developed under the reign of a sin nature. They were cultivated in hostile environments that did not know God nor His will. Yet, these very thought patterns are what we are using to frame our lives.

I began to realize how important it was that I allow the Word of God and the thoughts that govern the Kingdom of God to become my thoughts. No matter how *good* a thought pattern was, if it wasn't a '*God*' thought pattern, then it would not produce the will of God in my life!

By this time in my life, I wanted to see the miracles, signs, and wonders that God promised we would see. I wanted to see them on a regular basis. I wanted to see people set free. I wanted to have the kind of faith that believed all the things God has spoken over my life and the lives of others could, and would, come to pass. I wanted to be able to override all my doubts and fears by having a strong faith in God. A faith that took me beyond what my five senses detected to a place where it didn't matter what existed in this earth realm. I knew my God was not only *able* to do it, but He *would* do it! I realized, however, that my mind and my current mental structure would not allow my faith to grow to that level. My way of thinking, that 'stream,' was laced with fear and doubt. It was laced with a low self-image and intimidation. No matter how many great thoughts, words, visions, goals, and prophetic utterances fell at the top of my windshield (my mind), they all had to make their way through a contaminated, underdeveloped thought pattern, or paradigm. The life would be snuffed out of them before they ever had a chance to take root in my life because of fear, doubt, anger, or offense.

That day sitting in my car was pivotal to my life, my ministry, to understanding the very purpose that I was created! I began to realize that if I was going to do anything for God, produce anything for the Kingdom of God, I would have to *actively* go about changing the way I think! I would have to become a gardener for my soul, the manager of my mind. I'd have to identify those thought patterns that I lived with all my life that were toxic and begin to dismantle them and rebuild new ones based on the Word of God! After all, in the very beginning, in the book of Genesis chapter one, mankind was made in the 'image and likeness of God.' Well, if that were true, then there is no way we should be living defeated lives with no manifestation. We should be victorious and know how to overcome any obstacles that come our way. We should be people of joy and contentment – not because everything is right and good around us, but because we have a victorious mindset that understands that no matter what we face, we are destined to win because of our unique design and our relationship to our Great God!

According to Leviticus 25:8-10, the Jubilee occurred every 50 years. At that time, all debts were released and everything that needed to be restored, was restored. This is your 50-day journey to a 'mental jubilee.' Each day you will be presented with a fresh new way of thinking to help you dismantle old, toxic mindsets. You will be released from old traps and snares that have been constructed in your mind, and your thought patterns will be restored to a place that promotes victory, liberty, and the ability to walk in your God-given assignment in this earth realm!

Each day you will get an opportunity to reflect on the focus of that day. Then, in the 'Reflections' section, I encourage you to write down your thoughts and plans for freedom that you will receive from the Holy Spirit.

It is my prayer that this book will help you to become a manager of your mind. The days where oppressive thoughts that have stolen major portions of your day or week will be no more. You will learn how to 'think' like God thinks, to perceive the way that God perceives. You will begin to build new paradigms, ones that are built for mental success and that will produce the Will of God for your life!

Day 1

Think About What You're Thinking About!

"We use our powerful God-tools for smashing warped philosophies, tearing down barriers erected against the truth of God, fitting every loose thought and emotion and impulse into the structure of life shaped by Christ."
2 Corinthians 10:5 MSG

No thoughts that enter our minds should ever go unchecked. We must learn how to manage our minds and refuse to allow toxic thoughts to just run rampant.

Toxic thoughts are thoughts that are not in line with the Word of God and that are negative. These toxic thoughts are dangerous to our mental health, our physical health, as well as our spiritual health.

In our scripture text, God is commanding us to SMASH WARPED PHILOSOPHIES AND TEAR DOWN BARRIERS ERECTED AGAINST THE TRUTH OF GOD! There are so many thought patterns that God considers to be WARPED. The Holy Spirit, Who is sent to walk alongside us, reveals to us these warped philosophies and wrong mindsets on a daily basis. All thoughts that are rooted in worry or fear are warped! All thoughts of unforgiveness or those that initiate strife and confusion are WARPED!

Your focus for today is to ask the Holy Spirit to help you identify all of the Toxic Thoughts that may come into your mind and to ARREST them!

The KJV puts it this way: "Casting down imaginations, and every high thing (thought) that exalts itself against the knowledge of God, and bringing into CAPTIVITY EVERY THOUGHT TO THE OBEDIENCE OF CHRIST" (*emphasis mine*).

It's time to arrest some thoughts. Think about what you're thinking about, and make sure that you are actively examining every thought that comes into your mind. If the thoughts are outside of the Word of God, you need to arrest the thoughts and bring them into captivity. Let them know they are not allowed to take up mental real estate in your mind any longer.

Reflections:

_____
_____
_____
_____
_____
_____
_____
_____
_____
_____
_____
_____
_____
_____
_____
_____
_____
_____
_____
_____

Day 2

Be Always Ready!

"Our tools are ready at hand for clearing the ground of every obstruction and building lives of obedience into maturity." *2 Corinthians 10:6 MSG*

A good soldier is always ready and on guard in anticipation of an intrusion of their enemy. As Believers, we need to always be ready for an intrusion in our minds of unwanted and uninvited thoughts.

What an awesome scripture to live by: Always be ready and have our tools at hand to clear the ground of EVERY OBSTRUCTION. What mental obstructions try to invade your peace of mind? What mental strongholds try to stop you from living completely for God? Is there something in you that always trips you up when you try to make those purposeful steps toward your destiny? These are all OBSTRUCTIONS that Satan throws up to stop you, or at the very least, hinder your progress.

The second part of that scripture focuses on using our God tools to build lives of obedience into maturity. Our 'God tools' are the scriptures that we are to use against the enemy. We see that not only does skillful use of the Word defend our minds from unwanted invasions, but it also helps us to build a lifestyle of obedience *into* maturity. Isn't that what we are all striving for?

So what are those God tools? Do you have them **ready at hand** so that when the enemy comes to defeat you in your thought life, you can pull out the proper weapon to drive him out or back or away? The tools that we use are the scriptures found in the Word of God. Let's say for example the devil is bombarding you with FEAR. Your God tool would be 2 Timothy 1:7, which states "For God has not given us the spirit of Fear, but of POWER, LOVE AND OF A SOUND MIND."

Our God tools can only come from the Word of God; and when applied in our life, it will not only defeat the enemy who comes to plant lies in our minds, but it will cause us to live a life of obedience to His Word and cause us to mature in Him.

Glory to God! Isn't that what we're all striving for? Peace of Mind, an Obedient Lifestyle, and ultimately, Spiritual Maturity!

Get busy building your 'Spiritual Arsenal' Today!

Reflections:

Day 3

It's A Heart Thing!

"Keep vigilant watch over your heart; *that's* where life starts. Don't talk out of both sides of your mouth; avoid careless banter, white lies, and gossip. Keep your eyes straight ahead; ignore all sideshow distractions. Watch your step, and the road will stretch out smooth before you. Look neither right nor left; leave evil in the dust."
Proverbs 4:23-27 MSG

Your heart is not just an organ that keeps blood flowing throughout your body. Science is now showing that the heart has a brain. The brain in the heart and the brain in the head are, of course, closely tied together. The Bible has pointed to this fact forever! There was always the implication that the heart had emotions and an ability to guide you.

In Proverbs, we are encouraged to *'guard our hearts'* (KJV) or to *'keep vigilant watch over our heart'* (MSG). It is important that we watch and tend to the garden of our heart. We must watch what kinds of thoughts and paradigms are planted there. We have the responsibility to *uproot everything* that would contaminate our heart or cause us to make bad or negative choices. The Message Bible states, "That's where Life starts."

Every day we need to be pruning our hearts. I believe that within the confines of the 'heart brain' we find the place where 'core values' of what we believe and who we are, are stored. It is the place where 'automatic' responses come from. When we are faced with difficult or traumatic circumstances, or even carrying out automatic commands on a daily basis, our responses come straight from that core. If the core is corrupt, our decisions will be corrupt, our reactions and responses will be corrupt, and the normal flow of life will be corrupt. But if the 'core' is good and has been or is in the process of being renewed by the Word of God, it will produce automatic 'goodness' and Godly decisions and responses. The flow of life will automatically be in a good vein and will produce Kingdom results in our lives.

We must become managers of our hearts. Don't let unforgiveness, depression, defensiveness, or a critical or judgmental spirit, among other things, live in the core of your heart. *Pluck that stuff out!* They are deadly weeds to your soul! They destroy the life that is supposed to exist there, and they stop you from walking automatically in the attributes of a son of God!

Today, examine your every motive. Where are those attitudes and ideas coming from? Tend to your garden and uproot anything that hinders you from being who you should be – an effective witness for Christ.

Reflections:

Day 4

The 'YOU' View

"We were in our own sight as grasshoppers, and so we were in their sight." *Numbers 13:33 KJV*

Your self-image is closely tied to your success in life.

Moses had just sent out 12 spies to explore the promised land of Canaan. They returned with huge fruit from the Land and talked about its beauty and its lusciousness. Only one problem – they saw the giants (opposition to the promise) in the land. Because they had just come out of slavery for hundreds of years, they could not wrap their minds around the fact that this beautiful and lush land was God's promise for *them*. So instead of focusing on the awesome place that God was blessing them with, they *AUTOMATICALLY* focused on the opposition to the promise.

This is the same problem we face today. We come to know Christ as our Savior, and our lives are immediately translated from the kingdom of darkness into the Kingdom of His

Dear Son. EVERYTHING changes for us. We are suddenly children of THE KING! We become royalty. We gain access to power, wealth, health, and WHOLENESS. We have now left the kingdom of 'not enough,' of sickness and disease, brokenness and despair. BUT we bring that old mentality over into our new Kingdom. We even view this Loving God, our Father by adoption, as this judgmental being who wants us to suffer so we can love Him. That's because suffering was a huge part of that old system.

NOT SO IN THE KINGDOM OF GOD! We have a Good God. He is a loving, caring Father who gives liberally to all His Sons and Daughters. We need to get a revelation of WHOSE we are. We need a revelation of the fact that His Word says in the Psalms, "No GOOD thing will He withhold from those who walk uprightly." Matthew talks about seeking first the Kingdom of God and then ALL THINGS WOULD BE ADDED TO US!

How do you view yourself? Are you still viewing yourself through that slave mentality of your old life and existence? Do you see yourself as unworthy of the promises of God or fearful that those promises are too good to be true? Do you automatically focus on why you can't have them? Do you always look first at the opposition? Or are you getting a revelation of who you are in HIM?

You can literally look around your life and point to things that have not made the transition into this new Kingdom with you. Maybe it's your finances, your health, your family, your home. Whatever it is, you can declare: "_____ you must come into divine alignment to my Sonship! I know who I am – I am a King in my own eyesight and so am I in theirs."

Now, everything and everyone will begin to view you as the King that you believe yourself to be!

Reflections:

Day 5

Watch Your Mouth!

"Death and life are in the power of the tongue: and they that love it shall eat the fruit thereof." *Proverbs 18:21 KJV*

You have the power of death and life right in your mouth. You can either speak blessing or cursing over your life, your family, your finances, anything that concerns you, just by the words that you speak. Many times, without thinking, we curse a situation before we bless it. Have you ever found yourself saying things like, "I have more month than money," or "This asthma of *mine* gets worse every spring," or "my kids drive me crazy." These types of words have *creative power* that bring to pass exactly what you speak. You should never call any diagnosis 'mine.' It's not yours. God didn't give it to you. Don't call it '*my* diabetes,' or '*my* migraines.' Sickness and disease are a part of the curse, and you shouldn't claim it as yours!

We are created in the image and likeness of our Father; therefore, we are *Speaking Spirits!* We possess the ability to literally frame our world with our words! What do you want to see in your world versus what you are currently seeing? Do you want to see the blessings and promises of the Lord, or do you want to see the curses that exist in this realm manifested in your life? It is so easy for us to confess what we see, rather than to *change what we see* by our confession. If your marriage is going awry, or your kids are acting crazy, or your money is funny, or you're experiencing some kind of health challenge – search the WORD OF GOD and find a scripture that you can memorize and speak over that situation, and watch that thing turn around and line up with the Word of God! You have the power to do it right in your mouth! **You have to set yourself in agreement with God's Word and what it says about you, and begin to confess only that and nothing else, no matter how bad the situation looks!** Being raised in a 'Word of Faith' church, my pastor taught us about the power of our words. We wouldn't dare say things like, "I love you to death." Instead, we would say, "I love you to life." To some that may not seem like a big deal, but it is. Words have power!

The scripture continues to say, "they that love it shall eat the fruit thereof." This implies that you speak automatically out of your mouth whatever you are trained to speak, the way you *love* to speak. Now you may not actually love the negativity, but because you don't change it, you imply that you love it. And however you *love* to speak, blessing or cursing, you will see the 'fruit' or the 'manifestation' of it in your life. You cannot get around it. This is a principle of the Kingdom of God. Therefore, if you want good stuff in your life, if you want God's stuff in your life, THEN OPEN YOUR MOUTH AND BEGIN TO SPEAK IT!

WORDS HAVE THE POWER TO CHANGE YOUR LIFE! Use them wisely!

Reflections:

_____
_____
_____
_____
_____
_____
_____
_____
_____
_____
_____
_____
_____
_____
_____
_____
_____
_____
_____
_____

Day 6

What Are You Talking About?

"Put away from you false and dishonest speech, and willful and contrary talk put far from you." *Proverbs 4:24 AMPC*

"Don't bend the truth or say things that you know are not right." *Proverbs 4:24 ERV*

"Put away from you crooked speech, and put devious talk far from you." *Proverbs 4:24 ESV*

In Proverbs, we are given the instructions to put away from us a lying tongue and contrary ways of talking. God really does give us much instruction on how to develop Godly character throughout the book of Proverbs. I have given three different translations of this scripture just to make it plain.

In today's scripture, we are given the responsibility to manage our conversations. Take a good look at the conversations you are having. Are you a judgmental person, are you a gossiper, are you a person who is prone to sarcasm? (I call sarcasm Christian Cussing.) There are some people who use their tongues like a knife. They are able to cut other people apart just by the words they speak about them. Some will say, "Well, it's true, I'm not speaking lies." Maybe not, but God is instructing us through His Word to put these types of conversations far from us. Truth or not, this is not the language of the Kingdom of God.

Many people may have been raised in homes where the conversation was not always uplifting. There was a lot of judgment and negativity, and so they inevitably learned to communicate that way. But when we come into the Kingdom of God, we must learn a new way of communicating. *Now it's time to manage your mouth! Govern your conversations.* When someone comes to you with juicy gossip, choose not to partake of that conversation. When the opportunity comes along for you to lie or be deceitful with your response, choose to be honest. Every single day we have an opportunity to have conversations that will either bring glory to God or glory to the devil. Keep that in mind the next time someone is trying to engage you in an ungodly conversation.

Paul tells us in Philippians, "Only let your conversation be as it becometh the gospel of Christ" (Philippians 1:27 KJV).

We have to strive toward adopting the language of the Kingdom. Let our conversations be seasoned with salt, that it may be good to the hearer. Salt is an ingredient that adds flavor to something. It also preserves or saves things. It is used to melt ice. When we season our conversations with it, we can add a good flavor to an otherwise undesirable discussion. We can save someone by having Kingdom conversations, or we may be used to melt the icy hardness that may have grown around their hearts just by having our conversation seasoned with salt.

Having the right kind of conversations really does empower us. When we come to the understanding that our words, and how we use them, can actually dismantle strongholds of the enemy, we will be more cautious in how we use them.

Today, practice having conversations that 'becometh the gospel of Christ' and His Kingdom!

Reflections:

_____
_____
_____
_____
_____
_____
_____
_____
_____
_____
_____
_____
_____
_____
_____
_____
_____
_____
_____
_____

Day 7

Enlarge Your Borders!

"Jabez cried to the God of Israel, saying, Oh, that You would bless me and enlarge my border, and that Your hand might be with me, and You would keep me from evil so it might not hurt me! And God granted his request." *1 Chronicles 4:10 AMPC*

Jabez was not born into the best of situations; even his name meant 'sorrow maker' because he caused his mother great pain when she delivered him. Can you imagine being called sorrow maker all your life growing up? What kind of image would that put in your mind about yourself? It is no mystery that Jabez had some mountains to conquer especially where his self-image was concerned.

Perhaps you have faced similar things, either from your family members, authority figures in your life, such as teachers, even life itself can sometimes give us such tremendous blows that our self-image is low. We can't see how God could possibly bless us above where we are right now. And the devil will make sure that you keep that low self-image. He knows if you ever find out who you really are, nothing will be able to stop you from receiving all that God has for you!

Despite the negativity that surrounded Jabez, he had the boldness to pray one simple prayer. He asked the Lord to bless him and to ENLARGE HIS BORDERS. Most of the time we think it is wrong for us to ask the Lord to bless us. While we'll pray the house down for someone else, we rarely spend that amount of time or energy asking God to bless us. This is one of those strongholds of the mind that has to be broken. The Bible says, "Ye have not because ye ask not." If you don't ask for it, don't expect to receive it. The part I love is that Jabez asked God to enlarge his borders, and while that literally meant the land that he possessed, I also believe God had to enlarge his MENTAL BORDERS in order for him to be able to *receive* the blessings and the territory God had for him.

We need to ask God to enlarge our mental borders so we can have the capacity to BELIEVE that God wants to work things out for our good. Jabez was called sorrow maker all of his life, yet he was able to believe that God would bless him if he asked. He overcame the 'label' placed on him and walked in the blessing. We can do the same thing! No matter what labels society has placed on us, our families, or maybe even what we've limited ourselves to, if we ask God to enlarge our *mental capacity*, we can begin to see ourselves as God sees us. We'll begin to expand our self-image into one that will expect GREAT THINGS! If we feel good about ourselves, we'll expect good things to happen in our lives; and believe it or not, we will *attract* good things to ourselves!

I challenge you today to ask God to Enlarge the Borders of your Mind so that your level of expectancy for good things, for the blessings of the Lord, can increase. If you can believe it, you can have it! You're the only thing standing in your way!

Reflections:

_____
_____
_____
_____
_____
_____
_____
_____
_____
_____
_____
_____
_____
_____
_____
_____
_____
_____
_____
_____

Day 8

Becoming a Gardener for Your Soul

"So get rid of all uncleanness and the rampant outgrowth of wickedness, and in a humble (gentle, modest) spirit receive *and* welcome the Word which implanted *and* rooted [in your hearts] contains the power to save your souls." *James 1:21 AMPC*

Today's scripture text holds so much instruction for us as *managers* of our souls. Remember that your soul contains your Mind, Will, and Emotions. We have the responsibility, and we've been empowered by God, to manage our souls. We can look at our souls as a 'garden' that God has given us to tend. James instructs us to get rid of ALL uncleanness and rampant outgrowth of wickedness. Uncleanness or wickedness begins in our thought life before it is ever acted upon. Therefore, we must tend to the thoughts that enter our minds. It is our responsibility to get rid of those thought patterns that negatively affect our behavior. If we allow just a little bit of uncleanness or wickedness in our minds, it has the ability to contaminate every area of our lives. The devil cannot be contained. He may enter your thought life through unforgiveness, but he doesn't stay there. Soon you find yourself becoming frustrated, angry, unreasonable, and even sick in your physical body. Why? Because the enemy takes any entrance that you give him but doesn't stop there. That's why you must arrest every thought that comes into your mind that does not line up with God's Word and His Kingdom principle of Righteousness, Peace, and Joy in the Holy Ghost.

Our text today speaks of 'rampant outgrowth.' Doesn't that sound like a garden gone wild? That's exactly what it is. It is like a garden that has not been tended. You will find in this type of garden weeds will grow and eventually overtake whatever has been *intentionally* planted. In other words, we can plant the Word of God on purpose, but that's not enough. We must also *uproot* all the unprofitable thoughts that try to grow along with the implanted Word. Left untended, the weeds will outgrow the planted Word, and it will seem as if seeds (the Word) were never planted at all because you will see no fruit!

The scripture goes on to say, "receive and welcome in your garden (heart/soul) the implanted Word." Get that Word rooted in your life by studying it each day and becoming a doer of the Word. Remember the Word *Implanted and Rooted* contains the power to *SAVE YOUR SOUL!* The *SEED* has the power! We have to protect the Seed.

Today, I want to encourage you to do a little gardening. Look throughout the garden of your soul and root out every thought that is not born from the Kingdom of God.

Reflections:

_____
_____
_____
_____
_____
_____
_____
_____
_____
_____
_____
_____
_____
_____
_____
_____
_____
_____

Day 9

Does Your Life Prove the Will of God?

"Do not be conformed to this world (this age), [fashioned after and adapted to its external, superficial customs], but be transformed (changed) by the [entire] renewal of your mind [by its new ideals and its new attitude], so that you may prove [for yourselves] what is the good and acceptable and perfect will of God, even the thing which is good and acceptable and perfect [in His sight for you]." *Romans 12:2 AMPC*

We have been given the unique ability to retrain the way we think. Since God instructed us in Romans 12:2 to renew our minds, then that means He has given us the ability to do it. God does not want us to conform to this world, to be held by its customs and its ways of doing things. He does not want us to be bound by its systems. He has wired each of us with the capability of transforming our minds!

One of the major reasons people don't get actively involved in mind renewal is because they don't realize the whole point of a *renewed mind* is that it positions us to PROVE THE

GOOD, ACCEPTABLE, and PERFECT WILL OF GOD! Proving His will is what allows this world to see that the God we serve is Alive and Powerful, and He is at work to change things *supernaturally* in this earth realm through us, His children! However, we are incapable of proving His will without the process of renewing our minds. A person with an unrenewed mind simply cannot *believe* that the promises of God are attainable nor can they walk in the supernatural things of God. If you can't *believe* something, you can't *see* it; and if you can't see it, you can't *have* it!

I often liken the idea of proving that something works to a vacuum cleaner salesperson. If someone wanted to sell me an upscale vacuum cleaner, the first thing they would do is PROVE to me that it works. They would probably sprinkle some dirt on the carpet and let me use the vacuum so they can PROVE how good their equipment is. Well, it's the same thing in the Kingdom of God. We are busy telling people how good our God is, but have we really proven to them that He really works? How can we prove it, if it's not *working* for us? How can we preach God will bring you peace, if we're always in turmoil? How can we preach God is the healer, and we're always sick? Or God is the deliverer, if we're still bound?

The will of God is *GOOD*; it's not evil, broken, or twisted. The will of God for our lives is '*Soteria*' (wholeness), nothing missing and nothing broken! We have to renew our minds so that His Will can be seen through our lives. This world needs to *see* a God whose systems really WORK!!!

Will you actively engage in the process of mind renewal today so that your life will be living PROOF that serving our God does WORK?

Reflections:

Day 10

Take a Praise Break

"O clap your hands, all ye people; shout unto God with the voice of triumph." *Psalm 47:1 KJV*

Today is day 10 on our journey to our mental Jubilee! Let's take a moment to give praise to our God. He is worthy of all of our praise! Think about what He's done for you, think about where He's brought you from, He deserves our praise! The Bible says that God inhabits the praises of His people! He LIVES AND DWELLS within our praise. You want to be where God is? Then praise Him.

Every believer has to get the *revelation* of the importance of praising God. Praise has less to do with what's going on in your life and more to do with the goodness of our God! And He's good all the time. He deserves our praise! Even now while you're reading this message and going about your day, God is working something out for you! You are on His mind and He has a plan for your life. If you just get over into some exuberant praise, you will step into the breakthrough that you've been waiting for!

Sometimes we may have to give a *sacrifice* of praise. Hebrews 13:15 tells us, *"let us offer the sacrifice of praise to God continually, that is the fruit of our lips giving thanks."* There may be times when you feel like you don't have anything to praise God for. In those times, you just give Him a 'yet' praise. I may be going through…YET, I may be sick in my body…YET, I may be going through a financial challenge… YET, my kids are acting crazy, my marriage is on the rocks…YET WILL I PRAISE HIM!!! Sometimes we need to just confuse the enemy and offer God some radical praise right in the middle of our trials!

Remember in the book of Acts when Paul and Silas were locked up in stocks in prison with no apparent reason to praise God? It was about that midnight hour as they were praying and singing to God with the other prisoners listening on, that SUDDENLY there was a great earthquake, and the very foundations were shaken, and the prison doors opened. That is what our praise does! It shakes the foundation of our situations, and releases us from our prisons! It had nothing to do with their *feelings*, nor was there a natural reason to praise, but their praise preceded their BREAKTHROUGH! Praise is a weapon of warfare in the hands of a believer. It makes way for entrance of a spiritual invasion from the Heavenly Realm that will cause *SUDDEN BREAKTHROUGH IN YOUR LIFE.*

Wherever you are today, no matter what you're going through, take a few minutes to PRAISE THE LORD!! Everybody, Everywhere, PRAISE YE THE LORD!

Reflections:

_____

_____

_____

_____

_____

_____

_____

_____

_____

_____

_____

_____

_____

_____

_____

_____

_____

_____

Day 11

Grace: God's Empowerment!

But He said to me, My grace (My favor and lovingkindness and mercy) is enough for you [sufficient against any danger and enables you to bear the trouble manfully]; for *My* strength *and* power are made perfect (fulfilled and completed) *and show themselves most effective* **in [your] weakness. Therefore, I will all the more gladly glory in my weaknesses *and* infirmities, that the strength *and* power of Christ (the Messiah) may rest (yes, may pitch a tent over and dwell) upon me! 2 Corinthians 12:9 AMPC**

Thank God for His amazing GRACE! Grace is the *EMPOWERMENT* of God! Most of us are well aware of the saving Grace of God, that Grace that rescued us from a life of sin and death. But do you know about the other part of Grace that allows us to live a life EMPOWERED by God to overcome in the areas where we are weak?

As we are in the process of renewing our minds and changing our lives, don't ever think that we can do any of this just by sheer willpower. *No!* To restructure a paradigm takes an *empowerment* from God! If it was only based on willpower, all of us would be changed. We'd all be doing better. But to change a mind, how a person thinks or perceives things, requires the aid of the Holy Ghost! We need to ask the Lord every day for the Grace to make the necessary changes in our minds and our lives that we are seeking. Realize that we can't do it on our own nor is God expecting us to do it on our own. He has partnered with us for our transformation. He has given us His Holy Spirit, Who is the distributor of His Grace, and He walks beside us every step of the way.

Look at it this way, God is our Creator. He holds the blueprint for each of our lives. If anybody knows the plan for our lives, it's Him. He's knows what He has designed each of us to do and what it takes to carry out that plan. If there's anything in our lives that hinders that plan, He has empowered us by His Grace, to overcome it. For example, if He's asking us to walk in a new level of forgiveness, to let go of the past, that means His grace, His empowerment, has been released to enable us to obey what He's asked us to do. Employ that Grace!

Our scripture text says that His strength is made perfect in our weakness! I love that! God's strength is made perfect as it invades the weak areas of our lives. Where we are unable to make changes on our own, we have a Partner, Who is God's Holy Spirit. He gives us God's strength to be able to overcome! We are not alone in this transformation that we are required to make. He is with us, empowering us to do that which we are completely unable to do without Him!

Recognize the areas in your life where you need God's

Grace, His empowerment, to help you overcome! Remember, willpower alone is not enough. You need some power from on high to assist you in your transformation! Ask God today for His Grace, His Empowerment! He's made it readily available to you.

Reflections:

Day 12

God's Abounding Grace

"And God is able to make all grace (every favor and earthly blessing) come to you in abundance, so that you may always *and* under all circumstances *and* whatever the need be self-sufficient [possessing enough to require no aid or support and furnished in abundance for every good work and charitable donation]." 2 Corinthians 9:8 AMPC

Have you ever felt the Grace of God on your life for a situation that you were going through? Perhaps you have even said, "I don't know how I made it through that season of my life." Maybe it was the death of a loved one, a divorce, or some kind of financial crisis, and now that you look back over that time, you wonder how you made it through. You didn't make it on your own; you made it because God's Grace, His *Empowerment,* was on your life in order for you to be able to make it. His Grace had *abounded* toward you; it came to you just in the time that you needed it.

In the times when you are *Graced with Empowerment* from

God, it would almost seem like you are self-sufficient, as if you've got a good handle on the situation, and you're working it out on your own. That's how powerful His Grace is on our lives. Grace makes difficult and stressful situations bearable. People who are looking on from the outside may even say to you, "You are doing so well" or "I don't know how you do it." Well, you and I both know that if it weren't for the *Grace of God,* we would not be able to stand up under the pressure of most of the trials and tribulations that we endure. We'd all fall apart…if not for His GRACE!

I believe this is one of the ways that God demonstrates His love for us. He empowers His children with a special anointing called *'Grace'* and causes us to swim when we would have otherwise drowned. That empowerment keeps us running, when in our natural strength, we would have given up. You see, God doesn't always rescue us out of the challenging situations in our lives. No, He simply empowers us to be able to walk it out. Glory to God! Grace enables us to say, "I can do all things through Christ which strengthens (empowers) me!"

There is no task, no requirement, no assignment, nothing that God asks us to do, that we cannot complete, because He's empowered us. There is no situation that is allowed to exist in your life that you cannot overcome, because God has empowered you to overcome. Realize that it couldn't even come to us if He hasn't empowered us to overcome it. Whatever you are facing today, you are empowered by God to overcome!

You are a supernatural being! You've been empowered by a Supernatural God to carry out a supernatural assignment in this realm! There is nothing that can stop a person who is empowered by God's Grace – no trial, no test, no struggle, NO-thing! So move forward boldly today realizing that you've been *GRACED* to live this life!

Reflections:

_____
_____
_____
_____
_____
_____
_____
_____
_____
_____
_____
_____
_____
_____
_____
_____
_____
_____
_____
_____
_____

Day 13

Grace: God's Divine Power

"We have everything we need to live a life that pleases God. It was all given to us by God's own power, when we learned that he had invited us to share in his wonderful goodness." *2 Peter 1:3 CEV*

That divine power in the Greek is *'Dunamis'* which can also be described as *'the power of **grace**'* or the power behind grace. God has graced us to live this life. Our scripture reference today says, "We have everything we need to live a life that pleases God." This particular translation brings so much clarity to this verse. God's GRACE, or His empowerment, on our lives gives us the supernatural ability to live a life that pleases Him.

One bible resource defines GRACE as 'a dynamic force that does more than affect our standing with God by crediting us with righteousness; Grace affects our *experience* as well. Grace is always marked by God's *enabling* work within us to overcome our *helplessness*.' Isn't that powerful! Let's put it this way, it is God's 'super' coming on our natural, causing us to be SUPERNATURAL! Grace should affect our experiences. Grace should be *seen* in our lives, not just felt in our hearts. The world needs to see a people whose lives are impacted by a higher power, that power being the Grace of Almighty God!

This is how the empowering force of grace affects our lives. Let's say a person struggles with alcoholism. No matter how much they hate it, they simply cannot stop, even though it is destroying their lives and their family. It's bringing them to poverty and bad health, yet they still are not able to stop. But when the GRACE of God is activated in their lives, through prayer and faith, that Grace *enables* them to walk free of alcoholism. However, most believers don't tap into Grace at that level. They don't realize the power God has given to them through the Holy Spirit so that they can live a life that's pleasing to Him. Believe me, the only way we can truly be pleasing to God is to walk in the Grace that He has made available to us. The definition says it should affect our experience as well. Whatever is not pleasing to God in my life, I have been given the Grace, the empowerment, to overcome. Nothing, absolutely nothing, has to control my life! No addiction of any kind, no bad attitudes, no fear, NOTHING! If I walk in the Grace of God, then I am empowered to overcome anything that stands in the way of me pleasing Him!

Look at it this way, since He instructed us to live a Holy life, then He empowered us to be able to do so. That's the reason He can say that we are *'more than conquerors!'* That's why He guarantees our victory!

Whatever struggle exists in your life today, just remember you have been empowered by the Grace of God to overcome it. Declare the Grace of God over your life today, and believe that God has released it within you so that you can overcome! Every day say, "God, I thank You for the Grace to live this life today!"

Reflections:

_____
_____
_____
_____
_____
_____
_____
_____
_____
_____
_____
_____
_____
_____
_____
_____
_____
_____
_____

Day 14

A Superior Reality

"There is a way which seems right to a man and appears straight before him, but at the end of it is the way of death." *Proverbs 14:12 AMPC*

Did you know that there is a Superior Reality that exists concerning your life? Do you realize that all you see is not all that exists? There is a Superior Reality that exists in the Kingdom of God that supersedes all reality in this natural realm.

As Believers, we do not have to live our lives or handle our situations with the limited knowledge that is available in this realm. No. We have the ability to get wisdom and understanding from the realm of God's Kingdom. The scripture reference today says, "There's a way that *'seems'* right to a man but the end of that way is death (or destruction)." How many times have we made decisions or tried to figure something out only to have it turn out wrong? We used all the wisdom and insight we had, but it just didn't turn out the way we thought it should. There is insight and wisdom available to us from the Spirit of God that will cause us to be successful in our decision making and problem solving. All we have to do is pray and ask God for wisdom. He promised that He would give it to us in James 1:5 (GW), "If any of you needs wisdom to know what you should do, you should ask God, and He will give it to you. God is generous to everyone and doesn't find fault with them."

That's one reason why we should not just rely on our own thoughts and ideas when we need to make decisions. The Holy Spirit is our Spiritual Partner for this life. He has wisdom and understanding from on High. And when we seek Him regarding anything in our life or situations that we're in, He will give us a superior wisdom that will supersede any idea or thought we could come up with on our own. Let's face it, our own insight is limited and very often one-sided. When we engage the Holy Spirit, we open ourselves up to viewing things from a totally different perspective. It's like this, sometimes we can't see the forest for the trees. But the Holy Spirit's perspective is a bird's-eye view of the entire forest. From His vantage point, He can see the paths, the obstacles, the enemy, and the shortcuts. So while we may make steps in a certain direction because we *think* this is the next best obvious step, the Holy Spirit is trying to lead us in a different direction because of a 'superior reality' that He has based on His superior vantage point.

As you face challenging situations in your life, it just may be that the most *obvious* move is not the *best* move for you. Seek the face of God and let the Holy Spirit lead you. There may be a way that *seems* right to you, it may *seem* like a good move, but is it a God move?

Reflections:

Day 15

Exchanging Realities

"Let this mind be in you, which was also in Christ Jesus." *Philippians 2:5 KJV*

There is a way that God is trying to get His people to think. He tells us in Philippians 2:5 that we should have the same mind that Jesus has. Many Christians think this is impossible. They think 'we can't be like Jesus.' But the Word tells us we can be like Him because we can THINK like Him. And as a man thinks in his heart, so is he.

How do we develop that high place of thinking? Well, first we must study His Word. His Word mirrors His thoughts. As we read and study the Word of God, the Holy Spirit will give us fresh revelation into the mind of Christ. Now this is not trying to figure out how He thinks, it is simply exchanging a lower level of reality for a higher, more superior, level of reality.

What is the purpose of 'thinking like Christ?' I believe the main purpose for having the same mindset as Christ is so that we may see Kingdom manifestations in this realm. He said in His Word we would do even greater works than He did in the earth. How can we do greater works without thinking like Him? On our own, we can't even *think* of Greater Works! Also, considering the fact that we are Ambassadors of the King, it is a good idea to know how our King thinks. After all, an Ambassador is a representative of a higher authority or country. We are Ambassadors of the Kingdom of Heaven, and we have the responsibility to bring His Superior Reality into this realm. We are not to conform to this world; we are to be constantly transforming into citizens of the Kingdom of Heaven that represent Him well in the earth.

Through various verses in the Bible, we understand that we should live *in* this world but not be *of* this world. Yes, we do live here, but our thought processes and our citizenship are from the Kingdom of Heaven. So the *facts* that exist in this realm have no bearing whatsoever on the *truth* that exists in the Heavenly realm. Therefore, as I learn and align my thinking to the truth of the Word, then that becomes my new reality. The promises written in His Word become *truth* to me, and they override the *facts* that exist in this realm. The facts in this realm may say that my credit score will not allow me to live in a certain kind of house, but the Truth of the realm that I'm from says God doesn't need a credit score or anything else to put me in the home that He has for me! All it takes is the favor of God on my life and doors will open for me! Now, that is *not* to take away from the fact that adapting the Mind of Christ will cause me to strive to be fiscally responsible. The mind of Christ says that nothing shall be impossible for God. I have to meditate upon this scripture until it gets down in my spirit. Then, as it becomes a part of my new mindset, I am replacing the old mindset that says these things will never happen for me. I simply agree with what God has to say about me. I let go of the lies that I've believed concerning my life, that I can't do this, or I can't have that, and I embrace the Truth of His Word. If you let this mind be in you, it will change your Reality!

Reflections:

Day 16

The Mind of Christ

"For who hath known the mind of the Lord, that he may instruct him? But we have the mind of Christ." *1 Corinthians 2:16 KJV*

What an incredible statement to the Believer: "We have the mind of Christ." In most traditional religious circles, this passage of scripture is overlooked. But I believe it is one of the most important revelations to the Body of Christ. We must understand the fact that we have the Mind of Christ Himself. In other words, we have the potential to think just like He thinks, and we have the capacity to receive knowledge and wisdom from on High and use it in the earth!

Just imagine if the Body of Christ came to the place where we handled every encounter in our lives with the wisdom of Christ! It is possible! What an impact that would have on this world's systems. As we begin to destroy traditionalism and religious rhetoric from our core belief systems, we will begin to experience greater manifestation from the Kingdom of God.

The average Christian today limits God as to what He can and will do in their lives. Those limitations exist in our minds! God is no respecter of persons; what He has done for one, He can do for another. For example, a Religious mind makes us think that God allows sickness and disease to get our attention, but a Kingdom mind knows that in the Word, God uses His miracles and mighty works to get people's attention! He is the Healer of sickness and disease; He's not the author of it, nor does He need to use it to get our attention. We must get rid of these erroneous mindsets. They are hindering manifestation from taking place.

As your mind gets renewed, and you begin to exchange your worldly thinking for Kingdom thinking, your very life should be impacted outwardly as well. People around you should be able to see the results of a renewed mind in your lifestyle. You should talk better, walk better, and live better. Your automatic responses to situations that arise in your life should be more Christ-centered instead of self-centered. Why? Because we have the mind of Christ now. We are exchanging our worldly views and mindsets for Christ's mindset.

Remember the WWJD (What Would Jesus Do) saying that was so popular in the 1990s? What happened to that? It became just a rubber bracelet or T-shirt; the real meaning got lost in the hype. But that's a question that should stay on the mind of every Believer as we are renewing our minds and developing the Mind of Christ. WWJD is not a fad; it should be a way of life for the Believer!

Do you have the Mind of Christ?

Reflections:

Day 17

The Carnal Mind

"For to be carnally minded is death; but to be spiritually minded is life and peace. Because the carnal mind is enmity against God: for it is not subject to the law of God, neither indeed can be." *Romans 8:6-7 KJV*

To be carnal is another way of saying worldly, or of this world's system. It is also described as operating in the 'flesh' instead of the 'spirit.' Romans 8 warns us against having a carnal mind. It states to be carnally minded is *death*. Of course, that 'death' means a spiritual death or disconnection from God. Verse 7 goes on to tell us that the carnal, or worldly mind, is not subject to the law of God, neither can it be. What a dangerous place for a Believer to be – *carnally minded*. To have a mind that *cannot* subject itself to the laws of God places a person in the position of ultimate defeat in every area of his life. What an oxymoron, a Christian with a carnal mind. How can we call ourselves Christian but maintain a mindset that *cannot* obey Christ?

Every structure of thought that does not have its root in

God's Word will bring death or disconnection from the heart of God. To maintain a worldly viewpoint or perspective on anything invites this death into our lives. This is why we must be actively pursuing the process of *renewing our minds.* An example of a carnal mind as it relates to forgiveness is this, "That person has hurt me so bad, I could never forgive him." That attitude is based on a worldly system where self-preservation is key. However, in the Kingdom, it is the Lord who preserves and defends us. To hold on to unforgiveness causes undue stress on our minds and bodies, which eventually leads to all kinds of sicknesses and possibly even death. This is what God is trying to prevent in our lives. We have to let go of carnal, or worldly systems of belief, and embrace a Spirit-led, Kingdom-bred, mindset. It will set us free. Spiritual thinking brings LIFE to us!

In Deuteronomy 30:19, the Lord admonishes us to 'choose life.' He says, "I place before you life and death." What is He saying? You have two systems of belief before you: LIFE from the Kingdom of Heaven or DEATH from this world's system; Choose LIFE! Every day you are given an opportunity to destroy your carnal mind by making Spirit-led choices. Get rid of a carnal way of thinking which will bring you death and disconnect you from God! Employ a paradigm that is born out of the Kingdom of Heaven that will bring LIFE and freedom and liberty! Make this choice on purpose, every day, until it becomes your automatic way of thinking.

Today, He's placing before you Life (Spiritual Mind) and Death (Carnal Mind); *CHOOSE* LIFE!

Reflections:

Day 18

The Effects of Carnality on our Reasoning

"Now the mind of the flesh [which is sense and reason without the Holy Spirit] is death [death that comprises all the miseries arising from sin, both here and hereafter]. But the mind of the [Holy] Spirit is life and [soul] peace [both now and forever]." *Romans 8:6 AMPC*

Today, we're focusing on how carnality affects our ability to reason things out. Look at the first part of our scripture text today: the mind of the flesh is sense and reason WITHOUT the Holy Spirit. Carnal minds lead the Believer to a place of reasoning without the aid of the Holy Spirit Who is our Life Partner. Carnal thinking leaves us in a position to have to reason things out with our own natural minds, which, in most cases, can be destructive for us. Being that many of us are impulsive creatures, we get a lot of exercise 'jumping to conclusions.' Do you know what that statement actually means? It means that we skip over a lot of facts and reach our own conclusions with our limited knowledge and insight. I call it 'filling in the blanks.' This way of thinking has led to broken relationships, bad financial decisions, and missing out on great opportunities, among other things.

The scripture says that this 'reasoning without the Holy Spirit' is death. There are no profitable conclusions that can come from a carnal mind. Most times it leads to more confusion and takes us off the course that God has for our lives. The carnal mind has no connection to the Spirit of God, and therefore, cannot give us God's direction for our lives. The carnal mind is framed by this world's system. It's framed by our upbringing, good or bad. It's framed by the experiences we've had in our lives. Therefore, the carnal mind is corrupt in its nature. Depending upon the carnal mind to bring any level of success into our lives is a waste of time. The carnal mind is unable to think outside of the box that it's been framed in, and thus it has great limitations! The carnal mind is wicked at its root because it's based in this worldly system and can only produce what this system has to offer, death and destruction.

It's no wonder that we have to renew our minds and leave the carnal thinking behind us. If we are going to achieve anything in that great and glorious plan that God has for our lives, we must rebuild a paradigm structured by the Word of God through the Holy Spirit. For the Word says in 1 Corinthians 2:11, "who knows the mind of God, except the Spirit of God?" We need the Spirit of God to teach us and reveal to us the mind of God. As we make this transition in our minds, we will begin to see our reasoning impacted by a Godly paradigm. This will greatly affect how we see things and how we respond to them. The Holy Spirit can 'fill in the blanks' because He is the revealer of all truth. We can make better decisions and choices when we have truth.

Let's embrace the work of the Holy Spirit in our lives as we exchange carnal thinking for spiritual thinking! We want our reasoning to be according to the Spirit of God and not fleshly thinking.

Reflections:

_____
_____
_____
_____
_____
_____
_____
_____
_____
_____
_____
_____
_____
_____
_____
_____
_____
_____
_____
_____

Day 19

Carnal Thinking Leads to Carnal Living

"So then those who are living the life of the flesh [catering to the appetites and impulses of their carnal nature] cannot please *or* satisfy God, *or* be acceptable to Him. But you are not living the life of the flesh, you are living the life of the Spirit, if the [Holy] Spirit of God [really] dwells within you [directs and controls you]. But if anyone does not possess the [Holy] Spirit of Christ, he is none of His [he does not belong to Christ, is not truly a child of God]." *Romans 8:8-9 AMPC*

The carnal nature does not reside in the actual flesh but rather in the soul of man, in his mind, will, and emotions. However, it definitely affects the flesh. The 'flesh' is the part that carries out the dictates of the mind. Operating in the flesh is really giving in to the appetites and impulses of an *unrenewed* mind. God has given us the ability to deal with a carnal nature through His Word. The carnal nature has no choice but to change when it is constantly and consistently confronted with the laws that govern the Kingdom of God. As we begin to align ourselves to God's Word, we'll see a transformation take place. Our nature will become Spirit-led and that carnal nature will begin to disappear.

It should be the utmost desire of every Believer to please the Father. If that is your desire, then you will seek every way possible to make that happen, including crucifying or putting to death your carnal nature. You need to ask the Holy Spirit to reveal to you areas in your life that have a carnal root and uproot them! Is your attitude based in carnality? Is your perception based in carnality? Are your reactions based in carnality? What part of that carnal nature do you hold on to for your own protection? Do you have a sarcastic tongue? Is your mind filled with negative thoughts? Do you want to get back at people who have done you wrong? Are you the person everybody can come to because you have all the latest gossip? These are all elements of a carnal nature. These, among others, are things that cause you not to be pleasing or acceptable to God. They affect your lifestyle and your witness for Christ.

It is decision-making time. It's time for you to acknowledge that some of these things do plague you. You must admit that many times you do give in to a very carnal nature. If you've had times when you've said, "I admit it wasn't right, but I couldn't help it," you've yielded to that lower nature, and it has affected your life in a negative way. It is now time for you to let the Holy Spirit that dwells within you lead and guide you. It's time to give Him right of way with your responses, your actions, and your words. The only way this can happen is that you make the decision to yield to His promptings *each and every time* you are faced with a situation. You know when you feel Him saying, "don't say it that way" or "handle it this way." You must develop the *habit* of letting the Holy Spirit lead! And if you miss it, you must be quick to acknowledge it, repent, and move on.

Today is your day to Let God Lead! Doing so will lead you to a lifestyle that pleases God!

Reflections:

Day 20

Take a Praise Break

"We should be grateful that we were given a kingdom that cannot be shaken. And in this kingdom we please God by worshipping Him and by showing Him great honor and respect." *Hebrews 12:28 CEV*

It's time for a Praise Break! Today in our praise, we will focus on our GRATEFULNESS to God! We are grateful that He has accepted and brought us into such a wonderful and powerful Kingdom. Our scripture reference says, "a kingdom that cannot be shaken." Hallelujah! It is a Kingdom that has a firm foundation. A Kingdom whose King is the Great I Am, the El Elyon, the Almighty God, the Possessor of Heaven and Earth. His Kingdom is built upon a firm foundation and established upon His unfailing Word!

In this Kingdom, we cannot fail; we are always victorious no matter what circumstances we face. We are grateful because we can depend on our King! He is always there for us. His Word promises that He will never leave us nor forsake us. Just think back over the last year of your life, times when you weren't sure you were going to make it through. The enemy dropped some pretty strong bombs in your life – perhaps some physical bomb of sickness or an emotional bomb. Maybe you faced a financial crisis, and you simply did not know how you were going to make it out. BUT GOD… Your King stepped in, and He showed you a way of escape. He healed your body, or He delivered and healed you emotionally. You received a supernatural move in your finances. Whatever the case may be, our King deserves our praise today.

His unshakable, unmovable Kingdom is why we should handle every situation in the Realm of the Kingdom of God, because it offers stability and soundness in places of turmoil. When we try to handle it in this realm of instability and brokenness, we have no guarantee it's going to work out in our favor. But thanks, be to God, our Father and King, Who ALWAYS causes us to triumph in Christ Jesus! He deserves our High Honor and all Praise is due His name. Our prayer should be that our lives would never dishonor Him or bring a reproach upon His Kingdom.

Today, take a moment to really let the King of Kings know how GRATEFUL you are for ALL that He has done for you!

Reflections:

_____
_____
_____
_____
_____
_____
_____
_____
_____
_____
_____
_____
_____
_____
_____
_____
_____
_____
_____
_____

Day 21

You've Been Translated from One Kingdom to Another

"[The Father] has delivered *and* drawn us to Himself out of the control *and* the dominion of darkness and has transferred us into the kingdom of the Son of His love." Colossians 1:13 AMPC

Praise God! We have been drawn out of the kingdom of darkness and into the Kingdom of light and love! We are no longer under the control of Satan and his imps. God is our King! He reigns over us, spirit, soul, and body! Now we must learn how to live in this new Kingdom.

The way that we thought and processed in the old kingdom is not the same way that we should be thinking in this new Kingdom. The things that used to defeat us in the old kingdom don't have to defeat us now that we're in the Kingdom of God! We are Victors in Christ! That doesn't mean we won't go through some things, but it does mean that we have the power and all of Heaven behind us to be able to overcome! Glory to God!

No matter what you may be facing today, it does not have the ability to overtake you. You have been transferred out of its control and ability to win in your life. You are now in a Kingdom where you ALWAYS win. Your King is the Champion of ALL TIMES! In this new Kingdom, you can trust in Him to bring you out on top every time!

This new Kingdom is 'voice activated' and 'seed manifested.' You have to find a Word to stand on from the Bible and then open up your mouth and begin to declare what you want to see happen in your situation. If you think about it, this same principle worked in the kingdom of darkness. You have spoken things that actually manifested in your life. 'I don't feel well' or 'I can't ever get ahead.' You might not have been able to see how your words were linked to manifestation, but believe this, words have power!

In this new Kingdom, the Kingdom of God, we come to understand, and it has been demonstrated to us from our Father in Heaven, that Words contain the power to change things. He created the entire earth with WORDS! Now you can do the same. Use His Word to create a new and victorious life for yourself.

What can you identify right now in your life that needs the WORD applied to it? What have you brought over with you from the kingdom of darkness that needs to be defeated? What mindsets do you still have and operate under from that old kingdom that need to be dismantled in order for you to live victoriously in this new Kingdom? Once you have identified some of these things, go to work on them. Find a scripture to stand on and begin to speak it over your life or situation. Ask the Holy Spirit to help you identify some things and then follow His instructions on what to do to gain the victory over them!

Reflections:

_____
_____
_____
_____
_____
_____
_____
_____
_____
_____
_____
_____
_____
_____
_____
_____
_____
_____
_____

Day 22

Transitioning Into the New You

"**Neither is new wine put in old wineskins; for if it is, the skins burst and are torn in pieces, and the wine is spilled and the skins are ruined. But new wine is put into fresh wineskins, and so both are preserved.**"
Matthew 9:17 AMPC

We're going to take some time looking at one of my favorite people in the Bible, Mephibosheth. His story is found in 2 Samuel chapter 9. Why is he one of my favorite people? Because I think that he represents most of us. He was a person who was born into royalty, but because of situations beyond his control, he was not raised in the kingdom. He lost his identity and became crippled in the process of being saved. He lost who he really was. He was a descendent of royalty but didn't realize it or perhaps didn't know how to get back to it.

And we are the same way today. We are kings in the Kingdom of God and don't even know it. We are royalty and don't even realize it. Religion, in its attempt to *save* us, has crippled us and caused us to lose our true identity. It has made us blind to who we really are and all that is available to us.

Mephibosheth's maid thought she was saving him by taking him and running away. But what she did was put him in a place that was a lower way of living. The very name '*Lodebar*' is a word that means 'no pastures.' In other words, there was no place to feed there. No nourishment there. Nothing to keep him healthy and cause him to grow strong. It was a place that stripped him of his true identity and caused him to accept a lower reality. This lower reality became his lifestyle. He began to think like the people there, to act like the people there, and to live like the people there. It all became his new norm. And because it was 'safe,' it became alright for him. We all have to be careful of becoming a people who are afraid to find a new norm, take risks, discover a higher and better way of living.

Like Mephibosheth's maid, religion has caused us to conform to a powerless system of belief – one that disconnects us from a true relationship with our Father. Though it may call Him Father, the religious system doesn't really allow us to know Him personally or discover the loving Father that He is. It causes us to pursue a relationship with Him that is very distant and impersonal. But that is not at all the Father's idea. His idea is that we live in constant communion with Him. In Genesis, He walked and talked with Adam in the cool of the day. He was very relational and Fatherly, giving Adam instructions and fellowshipping with Him daily.

After the resurrection of Jesus Christ, we got that relationship back. We are once again connected to our heavenly Father. Jesus is the bridge that allowed us back into close covenant relationship with the Father. He has re-established our ROYAL STATUS by way of the Blood and has empowered us to be able to walk in it! Glory to God!

Take some time today to recognize your royalty! You are a citizen of the Kingdom of Heaven. Meditate on that fact today and begin to act like it!

Reflections:

_____
_____
_____
_____
_____
_____
_____
_____
_____
_____
_____
_____
_____
_____
_____
_____
_____
_____
_____

Day 23

Discovering the New You

"Therefore if any person is [ingrafted] in Christ (the Messiah) he is a new creation (a new creature altogether); the old [previous moral and spiritual condition] has passed away. Behold, the fresh *and* new has come!" *2 Corinthians 5:17 AMPC*

Glory to God, we are NEW CREATIONS in Christ Jesus! Our past is just that, the past! Imagine the changes that Mephibosheth had to make in his mind in order to live in the Kingdom versus living in Lodebar. In the Kingdom everything was different. There was a good King there. A King that was interested in the most minute details of his life. A King that had great provision for him, who was more than willing to give him everything he needed to live a good life. What a change of life that had to be for him. Coming from a place where he'd been surrounded by lack and deplorable conditions. Now, here he is living in the King's domain! There had to be a change in his way of thinking. He could not bring his old mindset to the King's domain and think that it would bring him anywhere close to royal living.

No, he had to learn how to live in the Kingdom.

That's the place we are all in as Believers. We have to discover our true identity and learn how to live, think, and act in this new Kingdom. Where do the instructions come from? They come directly from the Word of God, the Constitution of the Kingdom. Inside that Book is where we discover WHO we are and WHOSE we are. We discover the laws that govern this Kingdom and how to apply them to our lives. Just like Mephibosheth could not bring the laws of Lodebar into David's Kingdom to live by them, we cannot bring the laws from the kingdom of darkness into the Kingdom of Light. We have to get rid of old ways of thinking and living that used to work in the old kingdom, and we have to allow the Holy Spirit to teach us things that pertain to this new Kingdom. Not only will He teach us these new ways, but He will empower us to be able to make the necessary changes in order to live successfully in this new Kingdom.

I'm sure that Mephibosheth was assigned servants and caretakers who were responsible for getting him in shape to live in this new royal Kingdom. Can you imagine the things in his life that they had to address? I would guess they had to address every area of His life: the way he talked, the way he ate, the way he conducted himself. Every area of his life had to be impacted by this new way of living. This is the same thing that is happening to us as we are translating kingdoms. EVERY area of our lives will be impacted by this new Kingdom. And it all starts with how we think.

Today and every day, allow the Holy Spirit to show you areas of your life that are preventing you from living and enjoying a Kingdom life. He will act as an Assistant in your life to help you to let go of the past and past mindsets and transfer over to a new way of living!

Reflections:

_____
_____
_____
_____
_____
_____
_____
_____
_____
_____
_____
_____
_____
_____
_____
_____
_____
_____
_____
_____

Day 24

Practice the New You

"Keep putting into practice all you learned and received from me—everything you heard from me and saw me doing. Then the God of peace will be with you."
Philippians 4:9 NLT

Keep putting into practice all that you have learned! To live a victorious Kingdom lifestyle and reap the benefits of living in the Kingdom, you must put into practice all that you have learned. As you are studying God's Word or hearing the Word preached, you must put into practice the things you are learning. It is not enough for us to just hear the Word, we must become DOERS of this Word as well. We have to put it into practice.

You might have heard the old saying, 'practice makes perfect.' Well, it's true! As we put into action the new things the Word of God instructs us to do, we will see our lives change for the better. But we can't just do it for a little while; it has to become our lifestyle. Let's use forgiveness as an example. The Bible teaches us to forgive. We must adapt a lifestyle of forgiveness. This takes practice. In other words, every time I am offended or hurt, I must practice the art of forgiveness. I must train myself how to release people and things from my heart and let them go. This takes PRACTICE! Believe me, you will get plenty of opportunities to practice this. Something or someone will offend you or hurt you, and you will have the chance to put into practice what you have learned and been instructed to do from the Word of God.

The more you practice forgiveness, the easier it will become when you are hurt or offended by something or someone. What does this do for us? It makes us free and able to move forward in the Kingdom of God. We'll have open access to His power and wisdom. It will keep us in alignment to His will for our lives and empower us to overcome the attack of the enemy.

The scripture text goes on to say, 'then the God of peace will be with you.' I don't know about you, but I **need** the God of peace with me every day! I need Him when I'm feeling anxious or afraid, when I'm overwhelmed by life and situations. My constant practice of following His Word and allowing it to impact my way of thinking is what will bring me into that level of peace.

What Kingdom principle or instruction can you identify that you need to start practicing today? How do you think it will impact your life when you start practicing it?

Reflections:

Day 25

Be Careful HOW You Hear

"So pay attention to how you hear. To those who listen to my teaching, more understanding will be given." Luke 8:18 NLT

We usually hear the words 'be careful WHAT you hear' or what you're listening to. But our scripture text today warns that we should be careful HOW we hear. What an interesting choice of words. It's not always what we hear, but HOW we hear that has the most impact on our lives. This is the reason that we have to renew our minds. Our mindsets and paradigms determine how we hear or perceive things. A wrong mindset will affect HOW you hear a thing. And hearing something in a wrong way will affect how you respond and how you carry out the instructions you are given and will ultimately affect your entire life.

For example, a person who is offended will hear with an offended ear. If the structure of their thinking is laced with offense, then no matter what someone says to them, they will be offended by it. Someone could be offering constructive criticism, and the offended ear would not be able to receive it as such but would instead take offense to the advice, and therefore, disregard it.

I can remember being in that state in my life. For a long period of time, I had an offended heart and personality. It was hard for me to take constructive criticism or correction. Every time someone was trying to help me by correcting or advising me, I heard it through my offended ear. This caused me to disregard the advice or counsel. I had thoughts like, 'this is just the enemy' or 'the devil just doesn't want to see me move ahead.' Always blaming the devil for something I really should have been trying to change or address in my life. Instead of listening to the counsel given to me, I heard, or interpreted, what the person was saying negatively. I had to get rid of that mentality so I could deal with my issues.

The only way I could even admit I had an offended mindset was that it was revealed to me by the Holy Spirit. That's why we must ask the Holy Spirit to reveal areas in our lives that hinder the move of God. He is our Partner and will reveal the mindsets and thought patterns that don't allow for transformation. He will show the areas that affect HOW you hear.

Today, take a moment to ask the Holy Spirit to reveal to you any mental structures that may be affecting HOW you hear in a negative way. He may show you past hurts or disappointments. You may be offended like I was. But ask Him to reveal them to you, and then begin to actively dismantle those mindsets through the Word of God and obedience to the Spirit of God. You can walk in victory as you begin to hear on a more clear and more free level!

Reflections:

Day 26

Let Not Your Heart Be Troubled

"Don't let your hearts be troubled. Trust in God, and trust also in me." *John 14:1 NLT*

You probably have heard this scripture quoted at many funeral services. But I would like to submit to you that this word of encouragement from Jesus was intended to be used for far more than someone's homegoing service.

First of all, the 'heart' of a man is the part of him that contains his soul. The soul of a man is his mind, will, and emotions. The Greek translation is 'kardia.' It is described as 'the center and seat of physical and spiritual life. It is the soul or mind, the seat of thoughts, passions, desires, appetites, affections, purposes, endeavors.'

The Lord is letting us know that continuing in a place of being sad, disheartened, frustrated, agitated, and upset is not good for your 'heart.' He stretches it further to say 'let not your heart' as if YOU have some say as to whether you're going to be troubled or not. Well, if He puts the ball in your court, then you have been given the control as to whether you're going to be troubled or not. You get to choose! Remember this troubling is affecting the center and seat of your spiritual and physical life. How much leeway are you going to give to it? How much control are you going to give to the troubling things that are going on around you? Are you going to allow them to just overtake you? If so, they will affect your thoughts, passions, desires, appetites, affections, purposes, and endeavors. That's a large part of who you are and something that needs to be only under the direct control of YOU and GOD!

When you are going through troubling times, don't LET your heart be troubled. You believe in God, believe in Jesus. Have faith in Him that He is able to see you through. Have faith that the Spirit of God has a set of instructions and directions for you to lead you out of whatever it is you're facing. Though it may not be easy, or it may take longer than you anticipate, YOU WILL COME OUT! The pressure WILL be lifted. The Victory is Assured!

One of the most important things that you need to engraft into your paradigm is the fact that no matter what you face or what you go through, you know Your God has you in the palm of His hand, and His plans for you are GOOD and not evil!

One of my favorite sayings is from Joyce Meyer - "It may not be good while it's working, but it's always working for my good." Take that as a life motto for yourself. It may not feel good while you're in it, but you can believe that your situation is being worked out for your good!

Reflections:

Day 27

You Get to Choose

"I call heaven and earth to record this day against you, that I have set before you life and death, blessing and cursing: therefore choose life, that both thou and thy seed may live." *Deuteronomy 30:19 KJV*

One of the most powerful abilities, and perhaps responsibilities, that God has given to mankind is the right to CHOOSE! Our scripture text today says, "I have set before you life and death, blessing and cursing." God is giving us a pop quiz, and then He's giving us the answer. He said CHOOSE LIFE, CHOOSE BLESSING! "How can I choose life?" you might ask. Or how can someone choose to be blessed? One way to choose life is by the decisions that you make!

I hope that by this point on your journey you have come to realize that the way you think is directly affecting the way you live. I pray that the connection between negative and toxic thinking, and negative and toxic lifestyles, is becoming very clear to you. If you have been praying and carefully following the words of this devotional and the instructions given, you are becoming keenly aware of your toxic thought life, and you are actively in the process of changing the way you think. You are CHOOSING to think differently. You are CHOOSING to tear down one structure of thinking and replace it with new and good thoughts and mindsets that are founded upon the Word of God! You may not be all the way there, and it may not be an *automatic* thing yet, but it is on the way. You are building up an ability to CHOOSE right thinking. You are re-building positive and God-centered mindsets within yourself. These new structures of thought will help you to CHOOSE LIFE and CHOOSE BLESSING!

Isn't it powerful to know that you can *choose* a good life; you can choose to get rid of negative thinking? You can choose not to live under a curse, and you can choose to be blessed. How? By speaking and declaring these things over your life. By finding scriptures that go along with what you want in your life. The Word says in 3 John 2, "I wish above all things that you prosper and be in health even as your soul prospers." If your soul is starting to prosper, you can receive the fact that you will prosper and be in health. If your mind is being affected by the Word of God, and your thoughts are truly changing, you will see the results manifest in your life and your outcomes. Glory to God! The Word of God contains the power to change your entire life!

Today and every day, CHOOSE LIFE! Choose to follow the Word of God! Refuse to entertain vain conversations. Don't get caught up in the attitudes of this world's system. Don't allow envy and jealousy to lace the way you think. CHOOSE to get rid of any thought pattern that does not promote LIFE and LOVE! You are well on your way to victorious living!

Reflections:

Day 28

Your Life is in Your Mouth

"Death and life are in the power of the tongue: and they that love it shall eat the fruit thereof." *Proverbs 18:21 KJV*

Yesterday we talked about our ability, and even our responsibility, to choose life! Well another powerful way to choose life, besides our decision making, is to SPEAK LIFE! We can choose to live and be blessed by the things that we are SAYING! Our scripture text today says, "death and life are in the power of the tongue." They are wrapped up in what you're talking about! Are you speaking death or life over your situations?

For example, let's say you are facing health issues. Maybe you have received some kind of diagnosis from the doctor. Are you calling that disease 'my diabetes' or 'my asthma?' By doing so, you are taking ownership of this diagnosis and agreeing with what the devil is trying to place on your life. Whatever you add your agreement to through the words of your mouth, you empower to come to pass in your life. This goes for any area of your life that the enemy may be attacking: your finances, your family, your job, it doesn't matter. If you're just speaking negative things in these areas, you're going to continue to reap a negative harvest. Death and life are in the power of the tongue, and you shall eat the fruit of what you're saying. I don't know about you, but I want to eat the fruit of life and of good things. I want the fruit of good health and prosperity to manifest in my life. That being the case, I decided a long time ago to stop giving place to the devil through my negative confessions.

In Deuteronomy 30:19, God has placed before us Life and Death, Blessing and Cursing, then He said CHOOSE LIFE! How can I choose? I can choose with my words! I can choose by what I'm speaking over myself, my family, my finances, every day. Refuse to speak words of death and defeat. Refuse to choose cursing for your life. Don't come in agreement with what you're experiencing. Speak Life! Go to the Word of God and find a scripture to stand on that pertains to your situation and declare that Word over your life. It will come to pass.

Today, take time to identify areas where you have agreed with some negative things that are going on in your life. Maybe you've said 'I can't ever get ahead' or something as simple as 'if it's not one thing it's another.' You may be able to recall one of many negative sayings that you have adopted over the years. Well, today is your day to begin to turn those things around. Get them out of your day-to-day conversations and begin to speak LIFE! It may be difficult in the beginning because you're accustomed to speaking a certain way, but you can train yourself to speak differently, to speak positive, God-filled thoughts over your life and existence!

Reflections:

_____
_____
_____
_____
_____
_____
_____
_____
_____
_____
_____
_____
_____
_____
_____
_____
_____
_____
_____
_____

Day 29

The Way That Seems Right, Might Not Be

"There is a way which seems right to a man *and* appears straight before him, but at the end of it is the way of death." *Proverbs 14:12 AMPC*

For every person there is a way that seems to be the right way to go, or the right way to do something, but many times those paths lead to destruction. I know we've all gone down a path we thought was the right way to go, but it didn't end up so well. Anytime you have not dealt with toxic mindsets or paths of thinking, this is going to be the result that we can expect. To an unrenewed mind, wrong or toxic thoughts or perceptions are all we have to go by in order to make decisions, to respond to things, or to try to pursue and build relationships. And the fact of the matter is, these wrong perceptions will appear as 'truth' to us, and unless they go unchallenged by the Word of God through the Holy Spirit, they will remain 'truth' to us.

For example, at some point in my life I had taken on an attitude of inferiority. I felt like everyone else's opinion was better or more important than my own. It began with my feeling misunderstood when trying to express myself, which led to feeling like my viewpoint was not important. I would just let things ride, sweep them under the rug. This was destructive! I had developed an attitude of conflict avoidance. To me, it *seemed* right to just let it go, don't confront anything, don't ruffle any feathers. My thinking was that I was not going to stir up any strife, or cause anyone to become upset with me, because my opinion differed from theirs. I felt that I could keep down confusion if I just kept quiet. But that wasn't true. I can remember feeling very frustrated and even angry because I kept everything inside, not quite knowing how to deal with my emotions. To keep things inside *seemed* right to me, but it wasn't. It led to a lot of confusion and strife. Many times it seemed that there was even more confusion and strife than if I had just opened my mouth and said something. It was a very destructive mindset that I initially thought was good, but it didn't yield good results.

It takes the Holy Spirit to reveal a lot of these paths to us, because on our own we may not see that they lead to destruction. We may not realize that every time we go down these certain paths of thinking (remember the water stream on the windshield), they don't yield very good results. We need the Holy Spirit to show us the ways that we think and process that are producing negative things in our lives. The paths may *look* right, the way we think may *seem* right, but the end results are *not* right. They take us to paths of destruction, hurt, and confusion, for ourselves, and very often, for those around us. The Holy Spirit, on the other hand, has a bird's eye view of our paths and can determine very quickly for us when we're getting off course. We need to learn how to inquire of Him as to whether our thinking is off or not.

Put into practice a habit of asking the Holy Spirit to lead and guide you in your decision-making process. Acknowledge that some of the ways you think may not be right and are yielding unprofitable fruit in your life. Exchange your way of thinking for God's way of thinking, and you'll start to see better results for yourself!

Reflections:

_____
_____
_____
_____
_____
_____
_____
_____
_____
_____
_____
_____
_____
_____
_____
_____
_____
_____
_____
_____
_____
_____

Day 30

Take a Praise Break

"I will bless the Lord at all times: his praise shall continually be in my mouth." *Psalm 34:1 KJV*

Today is day 30 of our journey to our mental Jubilee! Time to take another Praise Break! Our scripture text today says, "I will bless the Lord at ALL times." No matter what is going on in your life today take a moment to give God praise. One thing I have learned over the years is that no storm lasts always. Things can look bleak one day, and the very next day they can turn around for you. Live your life EXPECTING God to change things for you! Expect it every day, and give Him praise in the meantime. We have to remember that God is FOR US! And if God is for us, then WHO or WHAT can be against us!

The Bible also says that praise is comely for the upright (Psalm 33:1). It is beautiful for the upright. As Believers, we must learn how to praise God regardless of what is going on in our lives. In the good times and the bad, the best of days and the worst, God deserves our praise! The Word of God tells us that He inhabits our praise. He draws near to us when we Praise. If you want Him to come into your situation, then Praise Him! That's where He abides. He lives within our praise! Glory to God!

What can you praise Him for right now? What has He done for you in the last week, the last month? What has He done for someone that you know? What testimonies have you heard about? You are alive and breathing today. So Praise Him! You have another day to bring Glory to His Name. You have another day to see Him work something out for you. Now live in expectancy today that He will invade your day with the answers and solutions that you need to every situation. He's watching over His Word to perform it in your life today. REJOICE!!!

I used to wait for things to happen before I would praise the Lord. I'd wait for the testimony before I gave Him praise. Not anymore! I've learned that God deserves our praise NO MATTER WHAT WE'RE GOING THROUGH! Because He's a Good Good Father! Glory to God! He always comes through!

The text goes on to say, "His praise shall continually be in my mouth." Not grumbling, not complaining, but HIS PRAISE! We have to learn that when we are tempted to complain about where we are or what's happening in our lives, to continue to offer up Praise to our God! We have to literally train ourselves to Praise no matter what. Resist the urge to murmur and complain, resist the urge to speak words of doubt and defeat! Praise Your God! Praise Him! He is worthy! He's working things out for you right now! He's rearranging things and moving on your behalf right now. Praise ye the Lord!!!

Today and every day, take a moment to give God an exuberant, heartfelt praise, especially if you're in the midst of a trial. Confuse the enemy by offering God your best praise today!

Reflections:

_____
_____
_____
_____
_____
_____
_____
_____
_____
_____
_____
_____
_____
_____
_____
_____
_____
_____
_____
_____
_____

Day 31

Get Rid of All Anxiety

"Be anxious for nothing, but in everything by prayer and supplication, with thanksgiving, let your requests be made known to God; and the peace of God, which surpasses all understanding, will guard your hearts and minds through Christ Jesus." *Philippians 4:6-7 NKJV*

We all struggle with anxiety from time to time. Anxiety is really a lack of trust in God to perform what He said He'd do. It is a fear about the future or the unknown. Whatever the cause of your anxiety, God tells us in our scripture text today to be anxious for NOTHING! Well, I'm sure you'd agree with me when I say that is easier said than done.

I remember when a spirit of anxiety was trying to take over my mind. It was during a particularly rough season of my life. The enemy was plaguing my mind with 'what ifs' and doubt and fear. I was good and saved, preaching the gospel, pastoring and all, and yet I was dealing with this spirit of anxiety. It came from a place of not putting things into God's hands and trusting the outcome. Some things I had absolutely no control over, and it was really starting to overwhelm me. I was driving home one evening thinking about the basketball game the Cleveland Cavaliers were scheduled to play that evening. An overwhelming feeling of anxiety washed all over me. I began to feel it in my chest, my heart started beating fast, my breathing escalated, and I wondered what in the world was happening to me. I heard the Spirit of the Lord speak to me in that moment and say, "If you don't deal with this anxiety, you will be on medication for it!" What a wake-up call. I declared in my car that day, "No, I will NOT be on medication!" From that day forward, I began to fight the spirit of anxiety with everything in me. I began to study and quote Philippians 4:6-7 every time that feeling began rising up in me. Not only did I quote it, but in my study of it, I found out that this was an *action* scripture. This scripture needed to be acted upon, not just quoted! So I began to pray, supplicate, and give thanks to God just like the scripture said I should do. In doing so, I felt that spirit of anxiety began to loosen and leave my life.

If you are experiencing even a little bit of anxiety over anything, begin to fight against it. It has to be unacceptable in your mind and life. It is an attack upon the peace that God has given to us to live in. It wages war against our ability to believe God for the impossible. Anxiety will keep you from your destiny! It is a toxic mindset, one that we should never ever accept as normal.

Wage war today against ANXIETY! Refuse to bow down to its aggressive advancement in your life. You do not have to fear nor be afraid. God is with you just like He promised!

Reflections:

_____
_____
_____
_____
_____
_____
_____
_____
_____
_____
_____
_____
_____
_____
_____
_____
_____
_____
_____
_____

Day 32

Prayer Defeats Anxiety!

"**Be anxious for nothing, but in everything by prayer and supplication, with thanksgiving, let your requests be made known to God; and the peace of God, which surpasses all understanding, will guard your hearts and minds through Christ Jesus.**" *Philippians 4:6-7 NKJV*

Today, we'll continue to wage war on anxiety. We'll take a look at the strategies that God suggests we use against it. The first thing He says is that we need to pray. As believers, prayer is one of our greatest weapons. The problem I have discovered is that a lot of believers don't know how to pray accurately. They pray as one 'beating the air,' meaning it's aimless. It has no real target.

Prayer should be *aimed* at something. Sometimes we can't see God working things out for us because we've not asked specifically what we want to see Him do. In the book of Mark, chapter 6, verses 47-51, the disciples were out in a boat, and a storm had risen on the waters. The Bible says that Jesus would have passed by them walking on the water until they called out to Him. We think Jesus is just going to magically appear in the midst of our problems and struggles without us calling out to Him. The Word says He was going to pass right by them. The NLT says in verse 48, "He saw that they were in serious trouble." What? He saw it and was going to pass them by? Yes, He was! Why? Because we need to dialogue with our Savior. We are told to call upon Him when we need Him. We need to be specific in our prayer life. Some Christians need to *develop* a prayer life.

I realized in my own life, the deeper I go in the things of God, the more of a prayer life I need. The more I need to honestly and openly let my requests be made known unto God! Stop hiding behind big words and useless prayers like 'God, I hope...' or 'If you see fit...' Those terms lack the FAITH you need in order to receive from God! The Word tells us in Isaiah 45:11, "Concerning the works of my hands, command ye me." Command the Lord? Yes, He is telling us to put a demand on His Word. Decree and declare His Word over your life and situations and do it with BOLDNESS! You will see it come to pass in your life! Glory to God!

Today, make bold and specific prayers concerning the things that have been causing fear and frustration and anxiety in your life. Be Anxious for NOTHING! But in everything by PRAYER!!! Become a person who is accustomed to a life of prayer!

Reflections:

_____
_____
_____
_____
_____
_____
_____
_____
_____
_____
_____
_____
_____
_____
_____
_____
_____
_____

Day 33

Make Supplication to the Lord

"Be careful for nothing; but in everything by prayer and supplication with thanksgiving let your requests be made known unto God." *Philippians 4:6 KJV*

What does the word supplication mean? In the Greek, the word is 'deesis.' It alludes to a person who has some type of lack or need in his life and is seeking or entreating strongly for that need to be met. It could also be translated 'to beg or to earnestly appeal.' It gives the idea that a person who supplicates is pushing all pride out of the way and earnestly asking for HELP!

Have you been in a situation in your life where you've needed to 'supplicate' before God for some situation that you or a loved one was in? Maybe you're there right now. Sometimes, in our attempts to 'faith' things out, we override this place of entreating God, of laying our hearts before God, and crying unto Him for what is really bothering us. We may feel that if we give voice to the situation, we may be empowering the enemy. But that is not so! When you supplicate, do so with this understanding: "I am crying out to the only one that is able to help me. I am crying out to God who is able to invade my circumstances with answers and strategies from on High!" Crying out to God, or entreating Him earnestly, does not demonstrate a lack of faith. On the contrary, when it comes from the heart of a person full of faith, it is actually putting a demand on the power of God and its ability to change any situation.

An example in the Word of God is found in 2 Kings 4:18-36. This is the story of the Shunammite woman who was given a child though she had been barren. Elisha the prophet had prophesied to her that she would indeed conceive and bear a son. Her response was "don't lie to me Man of God." Well, she did have a son and when he got older, he was working out in the field with this father. He got a severe headache and fainted. His father had one of the servants take him to his mother, and there her son laid on her lap and died. The Shunammite woman took him and laid him upon the prophet's bed. She then saddled up her donkey and went straight to where the prophet was. To everyone that asked her how she was doing along the journey, she replied "all is well" (open declaration of her faith). It wasn't until she got to the Prophet Elisha that she broke down and fell to his feet weeping, telling him of her problem (supplication). You see, when she got to the one that was able to HELP her, she asked *earnestly* for help. She was desperate for an answer. She made supplication to the prophet! God heard her, and the prophet went to her home and raised her son up.

This did not show a lack of faith on the woman's part but rather her strong faith. She knew that the only one that could help her was the Prophet of God. Going to God, earnestly beseeching Him on behalf of some situation or person or for yourself, is not showing a lack of faith, but rather showing a strong faith in God and Him being the only One that is able to 'fix' this.

Glory to God! If you find yourself right now in a hard place, or maybe you are believing God on behalf of someone else, a loved one or a friend, don't be afraid to ask God, earnestly beseeching Him and crying out to Him, for what you really want. Pour out your heart to Him. He will answer!

Reflections:

_____
_____
_____
_____
_____
_____
_____
_____
_____
_____
_____
_____
_____
_____
_____
_____
_____
_____
_____
_____

Day 34

Come Boldly to God

"Therefore let us [with privilege] approach the throne of grace [that is, the throne of God's gracious favor] with confidence *and* without fear, so that we may receive mercy [for our failures] and find [His amazing] grace to help in time of need [an appropriate blessing, coming just at the right moment]." *Hebrews 4:16 AMP*

We are instructed to come BOLDLY, with privilege, to God's throne of grace. In the last chapter, we discussed coming to God with supplication, and that meant earnestly beseeching God on behalf of some issue or situation that you may be facing. In order not to misunderstand what this means, Hebrews tells us to come BOLDLY and with privilege. Come to Him like you know who you are and Who He is to you! When you pray to Him earnestly, crying out to Him, you're doing it in a way that depicts your awareness of Who God is to you and just how much He cares about you and whatever it is you're facing.

The scripture text today goes on to say, "Do it with

confidence and without fear." When we go to God in prayer on a matter, we must do it with confidence and not in fear. We must go before Him with an expectation that He's going to do something about whatever it is we're facing. God instructs us to do this because many times believers may feel that they've done something to cause the situation they're in, that they somehow deserve what they're getting. But the truth of the matter is, if you are standing righteously before God, it doesn't matter if you've caused your situation or not; Your God, your Heavenly Father, will hear and answer your prayer. He says that you will find mercy and grace just at the right moment. Another translation says, "just when you need it!"

As Believers, we must realize there is absolutely nothing that goes on in our lives that God does not care about. He says that the very 'hairs on our head are numbered.' Don't ever let anyone make you think God doesn't care about your situations, big or small, because He does. When you are faced with a problem, don't be afraid to go to God and ask Him to meet your need. He's your Father, He's your God. He loves you and is concerned about you. This is what supplication is all about. You can BOLDLY go to your Daddy (God) and ask Him for whatever it is that you need.

Just like a good earthly father, God would move heaven and earth to make sure that His children are all right. I have personally witnessed my husband go to great lengths to ensure that our family was well taken care of. If my children had a problem or an issue, they could go to their dad with full confidence that 'daddy will work it out' or show them how. He has proven himself to them. Let God, your Heavenly Father, prove to you that He loves you and cares about you. Go to Him Boldly, make your petitions known unto Him. Be bold, open your mouth and tell God exactly what's bothering you, and you will see Him move on your behalf!

Reflections:

Day 35

Develop a Heart of Thanksgiving

"Be careful for nothing; but in every thing by prayer and supplication with thanksgiving let your requests be made known unto God." *Philippians 4:6 KJV*

Another step we should take when we are dealing with anxiety is 'Thanksgiving.' "What in the world does that have to do with anxiety?" you might ask. It must have a lot to do with it, because God adds it to the list of things that we should do when we are feeling anxious or worried about something. The Greek word for thanksgiving is 'eucharistia.' By definition, it implies an outpouring of grace and good feelings of wellbeing that flow from our hearts. Isn't that something, that God would want us to have good feelings of wellbeing in the midst of going through a situation that is causing fear or anxiety in our hearts? The connotation here is that as exuberantly as you have asked God for something, it is the same exuberance that is expected in your thanksgiving.

Thanking God in advance demonstrates our faith in Him. In our scripture text, we are told to pray and make supplication with thanksgiving. This is going on all at the same time, which means the answer has not manifested yet, but I'm going to praise and thank God anyhow. I'm going to express my faith in His ability to answer, while thanking Him exuberantly in advance. It might seem crazy to those watching you, but you praise God anyway. If you're expecting a BIG answer from God, you need to offer up a BIG praise of thanksgiving to Him!

Thanking God in advance shows that you are standing in expectancy that He's about to do something great on your behalf. You may not know what it is or how He's going to do it, but you EXPECT that He will intervene on your behalf.

For example, if someone owns a grocery store and you're in need of food, and that person says, "Come by the store tomorrow and fill up your shopping cart. Whatever you fit in the cart is yours and you don't owe me anything." You would begin to thank that person right then and there, without having received one thing! Why? Because you know that they own the store and if they said it, you can have it. Well, how much more trust should we put in our God? If He said it about you, you can have it; it's yours. Even before you ever get anything in your hands or any manifestation in your situation, you can begin to thank Him, because He owns it all and He will come through! No matter what the need is: financial, health, peace of mind, favor; it doesn't matter. He owns the storehouse, and He's given you access to it! Thank Him, Praise Him. You can expect Him to come through for you!

Today, as you make your petitions known unto God, increase your faith; stand in expectancy of what God will do. Give Him an exuberant praise of thanksgiving! And every time you feel that anxiety level start to rise again, just begin to thank God for the answer!

Reflections:

_____
_____
_____
_____
_____
_____
_____
_____
_____
_____
_____
_____
_____
_____
_____
_____
_____
_____
_____
_____

Day 36

Receive the Peace of God!

"And God's peace [shall be yours, that tranquil state of a soul assured of its salvation through Christ, and so fearing nothing from God and being content with its earthly lot of whatever sort that is, that peace] which transcends all understanding shall garrison and mount guard over your hearts and minds in Christ Jesus." *Philippians 4:7 AMPC*

It is a wonderful thing to be in the Peace of God! One definition says "the Messiah's peace." One thing I realize is that everything God has given us is a piece of His own: His love, His power, His presence, His grace, and His PEACE. God's peace is a force. It carries with it the ability to destroy every place of unrest and anxiety in our souls. It's not like earthly peace that only comes when things are going well around us. No, this peace causes us to rest in the midst of a storm. It's the peace that Jesus had when He slept in the back of the boat while it was in the middle of the stormy sea and the disciples were so afraid.

Our scripture describes it as "that tranquil state of a soul assured of its salvation through Christ, so fearing nothing from God." Can you imagine living in such a tranquil state that you fear nothing? Nothing bothering you. Although there is chaos all around, you're in a place of peace and rest. That's where God wants us to be. The text goes on to say "it transcends all understanding." That means you won't even understand why you're walking in the level of peace that you're in. People may even accuse you of 'sticking your head in the sand' or 'you just don't seem to care.' But it's not that, you are simply immersed in the Peace of God! Hallelujah! The scripture says that His peace will "garrison and mount guard over your heart and your minds in Christ Jesus!" Glory to God! That level of peace promises to guard our hearts and minds. It will stand like a Roman Soldier daring any anxiety to try and enter in. Peace will stand guard and garrison (the troops stationed in a fortress or town to defend it) over our souls! That's why you know PEACE is a FORCE, not just a feeling!

We have to let this peace in though. Peace doesn't just come in the midst of a storm. We first have to do the things that God said to do in Philippians 4:6. We must pray, make supplications (specific requests), and offer thanksgiving to God. Then we can allow the peace of God to come into us and overtake us. This level of peace only comes because you know that you've prayed, and you're going to allow God to handle the rest!

Reflections:

Day 37

God Tells Us How to Think

"For the rest, brethren, whatever is true, whatever is worthy of reverence *and* is honorable *and* seemly, whatever is just, whatever is pure, whatever is lovely *and* lovable, whatever is kind *and* winsome *and* gracious, if there is any virtue *and* excellence, if there is anything worthy of praise, think on *and* weigh *and* take account of these things [fix your minds on them]." *Philippians 4:8 AMPC*

The wonderful thing about our Heavenly Father is that He not only tells us *what to do*, He tells us *how to do it!* I love that. He leaves nothing to chance. In our scripture text for today, God tells us *what* to think on. He is saying for all the other thoughts that you have, after you have prayed and given thanks to God on a matter, think like this.

Our divine design was made for love and good things. We were not designed to house negativity and chaos. We have to learn how to pull down those things in our mind and erect a good and positive structure of thought. We do that through the Word of God. Find a scripture to stand on, declare it over your life and situation, and don't stop until something changes and you see results. If you're in the midst of something right now, go to God and pray, and release your faith. Then allow the peace of God, that tranquil state of being, to cover you like a blanket.

The next thing God instructs us to do is to change our thought focus. Your 'thought focus' is the thing that you are focusing most of your time thinking on. You can't receive His peace if you continue to think on the negative things. Instead, replace those thoughts with 'whatever is true.' Now the 'true' thought is that you are healed, or delivered, or whatever it is that you are believing God for. You may be living out 'facts' right now, but the 'truth' will override those 'facts' if you just continue in your faith! So believe and confess what is 'true' about your situation, not the facts. He says to think on whatever is reverent and honorable and seemly. Get rid of the stinking thinking that is not seemly. What thought patterns do you have that invite anxiety or frustration? Whatever they are, get rid of them. "How?" you may ask. By doing just what 2 Corinthians 10:5 tells us to do: 'casting down imaginations and every high thing' or 'high thought' that is trying to become larger in your life than the truth of the Word of God. You have to literally cast down the thoughts, refuse to accept them, and then replace them with thoughts of peace and faith in God!

The scripture goes on to say we should think on whatever is just and pure and lovely and loveable and kind and gracious – those are all *good* thoughts. You have to practice thinking good thoughts. Why? Because evil and negative patterns of thought are always readily available, they're all around us.

It's not easy to think well when you are troubled; that's why you have to cast down the evil thoughts. God says if there is any virtue (moral goodness), any excellence, anything worthy of praise, *THINK ON THESE THINGS.* Our Heavenly Father is trying to train us how to think. You might say, "Well, there's nothing good going on to think about." The Word of God is good, and it's full of good things. Go to the Psalms or Proverbs and begin feeding your soul with good things.

Here's a challenge that I give to you today. Go to the Proverbs and read one chapter every day for 31 days straight. Read them in different versions, but read one every day. Journal what the Holy Spirit speaks to you over those 31 days. You will find that your thought life will begin to change for the better!

Reflections:

Day 38

Fix Your Mind

"For the rest, brethren, whatever is true, whatever is worthy of reverence *and* is honorable *and* seemly, whatever is just, whatever is pure, whatever is lovely *and* lovable, whatever is kind *and* winsome *and* gracious, if there is any virtue *and* excellence, if there is anything worthy of praise, think on *and* weigh *and* take account of these things [fix your minds on them]." *Philippians 4:8 AMPC*

Today, we will take another look at Philippians 4:8 and focus on that very last statement, "fix your minds on them." This is where the work of changing mental paradigms comes in. You have to FIX your mind on these things. You cannot allow your mind to just run rampant and think whatever it wants to think. You have to gain control over it. He has given us the power and ability to do just that. We have control over what we think. We must fix our mind on Him.

In Daniel chapter 10, in the Amplified Version, it says of

Daniel: "For from the first day that you set your mind and heart to understand and to humble yourself before God, your words were heard." Daniel had to set his mind and his heart to understand the Word of God. There will be a lot of things that will come to try and stop us from setting our hearts to understand what God is doing. Our five senses have been trained with thought patterns and mindsets that are not rooted in faith. So we tend to believe in the 'facts' that are presented to us, and that makes the Word of God, the Truth of God, of no effect in our lives. But if we would turn away from the thoughts given to us through this world's system of belief and trust what God says, we will find ourselves developing a mindset fixed on God!

When I was going through high times of anxiety, I had to find scriptures that would help me to resist what my mind was telling me. I would declare those scriptures every day, and throughout each day, until they became a part of my belief system. I was serious about 'fixing' my heart and mind on good and God-filled thoughts. Every time a negative thought would arise, or a thought made me anxious, I would say my scripture out loud. For example, "Psalms 27:13 promises I will see the goodness of the Lord in the land of the living." I was 'fixing' my heart and mind on God! I was training myself to let God's way of thinking replace my way of thinking.

This is not an easy process nor is it quick. But if you would be consistent in confessing the Word of God, the Truth, over your situation, you will find yourself with your mind set and unmovable. You will begin to believe that what the Word says is true and that it will change your situation. Today 'fix' your heart and your mind on God!

Reflections:

_____
_____
_____
_____
_____
_____
_____
_____
_____
_____
_____
_____
_____
_____
_____
_____
_____
_____
_____
_____

Day 39

God Says, 'Don't Worry'

"So don't worry about these things, saying, 'What will we eat? What will we drink? What will we wear?' These things dominate the thoughts of unbelievers, but your heavenly Father already knows all your needs. Seek the Kingdom of God above all else, and live righteously, and he will give you everything you need. So don't worry about tomorrow, for tomorrow will bring its own worries. Today's trouble is enough for today."
Matthew 6:31-34 NLT

God is constantly dealing with our souls (mind, will, and emotions). In our text today, He is saying don't worry about what you're going to eat or what you're going to put on. He says, "these things dominate the thoughts of unbelievers." Believers are supposed to know beyond the shadow of a doubt that God is going to take care of them. Most of us, however, don't always operate that way. We fret and worry over what we don't have, what doesn't seem to be enough. We have not trained our minds to believe the 'Kingdom way.'

Verse 33 says, "seek the Kingdom of God above all else." We are to seek God's way of doing things and then adapt it as our own. He has always promised to take care of us. As a matter of fact, in the Psalms, David states that he has "not seen the righteous forsaken, nor His seed begging bread" (Psalms 37:25). The Amplified Bible describes it this way, 'the uncompromisingly righteous.' Glory to God! Once you have made up your mind to live righteously and you are walking in the ways of God, you can *expect* God to take care of your every need. He promised it in His Word! God has made a covenant with us, and His part says that He will take care of us. He will meet every need.

The Word tells us that thoughts of lack, of not having enough, these troubling thoughts belong to unbelievers, those who have no relationship with our loving Heavenly Father. But once you are a part of the Kingdom of God, you should no longer be dominated by those kinds of thoughts. You should not spend your days and nights worrying about provision, healing, or anything else. You have to learn to trust in your King, your Father. Trust that He loves you and that if He takes care of the grass in the field and the birds in the air, surely He will take care of you!

God says, "Don't worry about tomorrow, for tomorrow has cares of its own." He says His Grace is sufficient to keep us. We talked about that back on Day 11 of this devotional. His Grace will cover and keep us through whatever we must face. That is why we don't have to fear or worry. We can be fully persuaded in His ability to come through for us, no matter what! He says, "When you seek My Kingdom FIRST, I'll *automatically* give you everything you need." Because He knows what we need even before we ask.

What a comfort to be part of a Kingdom with such a wonderful King, Whose heart is toward His people in meeting their every need. That's the Kingdom of God, the Kingdom you and I are a part of!

Reflections:

_____
_____
_____
_____
_____
_____
_____
_____
_____
_____
_____
_____
_____
_____
_____
_____
_____
_____
_____
_____

Day 40

Take a Praise Break

"Taste and see that the Lord is good. Oh, the joys of those who take refuge in him!" *Psalms 34:8 NLT*

We've now spent several days fighting against spirits of anxiety, worry, and fear. Now it's time to rejoice because God is setting us free from their entrapment! We now know that we can live free from those things; and *if* they try to come back, we know that we have authority over them through the Word of God!

Our text says, "Taste and See that the Lord is good!" We've tasted of the goodness of the Lord through His Word for almost 40 days now. We've taken time to dissect His Word, to eat at His table, to reflect on our lives and situations. Now it's time to praise God for all that He has done for us!

The scripture says, "Oh, the joys of those who take refuge in Him!" As we take refuge in Him, His joy floods our soul. That's the whole point. When we feel anxious or worried, take refuge in Him and allow Him to fill our souls with joy!

Rejoice, rejoice, despite how you may be feeling today. Offer a sacrifice of praise unto Him! It is in the release of your praise that you will feel that joy! For the Lord our God is a good, good Father! He loves us so much and has made perfect provision for whatever we may be in need of. There is no need to fear nor to worry. He will never leave us nor forsake us!

Today, give a loud, boisterous praise unto the Lord! A shout of VICTORY over anxiety! Declare yourself free, and walk in that freedom. For GREAT is our GOD and GREAT is His PEACE in our lives!

Reflections:

_____
_____
_____
_____
_____
_____
_____
_____
_____
_____
_____
_____
_____
_____
_____
_____
_____
_____
_____

Day 41

Great Minds Don't Think Alike!

"Thank you for making me so wonderfully complex! Your workmanship is marvelous—how well I know it." Psalms 139:14 NLT

God created each of us with a unique design. Though we were all born in His image and likeness, He also placed within us a unique design that is our very own. Although you may have heard the saying "great minds think alike," I beg to differ and say "great minds really don't think alike."

In the uniqueness of our design, God has placed giftings and talents within us. He expects that we would tap into them and use them to fulfill our earthly assignments. All too often, we fall into the dangerous trap of trying to be a duplicate of someone we admire and look up to. Though these people may be an inspiration to us, God never intended for there to be two of them in the earth. We each have been placed in the earth for a specific purpose; and if we try to live out someone else's destiny, we'll never reach our own.

I can remember going through times as a minister, preaching the Word, where the 'style' of someone's preaching was intriguing to me. I would try to incorporate their style into my style, and it never worked. I had to come to the conclusion that God had designed me to minister in a certain way. To try and do it any other way was literally telling God that He'd made a mistake in my unique design.

Great minds simply cannot think alike. We're not designed that way. In the same way that we can't duplicate someone, we can't expect others to become duplicates of us. If you're a parent, you may fall into the trap of trying to make your children like you. While they may have certain traits like us, the fact of the matter is, they have their own unique design as well. Let us not put the pressure on others to be 'like' us. First, we rob them of carrying out the plan and purpose for their lives; and second, we put them in a very uncomfortable position of trying to be something they simply were not designed to be.

Today, free yourself from the confines that you may have placed on yourself by trying to be like someone you admire. Then, free others from the restraints and demands to be like you. We've all been fearfully and wonderfully designed by God for His purposes; therefore, to be anything other than who we were designed to be is an insult to our Creator!

Be the YOU that you were created to be!

Reflections:

Day 42

#TeamMe!

"Don't copy the behavior and customs of this world, but let God transform you into a new person by changing the way you think. Then you will learn to know God's will for you, which is good and pleasing and perfect."
Romans 12:2 NLT

Generally, we are encouraged to prefer others above ourselves. But there comes a time in all of our lives that we must think of ourselves as well. God requires all of us to make changes in our lives. The things that He points out by the Holy Spirit, He also gives us the ability to change. In our scripture text today, He tells us to not copy the behavior and customs of the world, but let God transform us into a new person by changing the way we think! We have now spent time challenging many of the mindsets we have. We have examined them and been challenged to change the way we think, so that our thinking lines up with God's thinking.

Each year in our women's ministry, I open with a teaching called #TeamMe! This campaign encourages women to discover who they are in Christ and to identify things in their lives that hinder them from becoming what God created them to be. We look at things like: bad attitudes, being offended, pain from past situations, forgiveness, and learning how to accept God's healing, love, and forgiveness. We take the time to dig through the rubble of our souls and allow God to heal us. During these times of ministry, it is important that our focus turns within. We have to be able to honestly look within ourselves and ask the Holy Spirit to reveal the areas in our lives that hinder us from moving forward. That's why it's called Team Me.

Over the years, #TeamMe has become an ongoing venture for us. We are now in the habit of making changes to the way we think. We are constantly working on ourselves; and for just a little while, we make ourselves and our transformation a priority in our lives. Our ultimate goal is to become exactly what God wants us to be.

Join our #TeamMe campaign and make your transformation a number one priority in your life. It is the intent of God that we learn and walk out His will for us. We can only do that as we disconnect from the behaviors and customs of this world and transform into true Kingdom citizens. For once, it is all about YOU!

Reflections:

_____
_____
_____
_____
_____
_____
_____
_____
_____
_____
_____
_____
_____
_____
_____
_____
_____
_____
_____
_____

Day 43

We Have the Power to Transform!

"I pray that you will begin to understand how incredibly great his power is to help those who believe him. It is that same mighty power that raised Christ from the dead and seated him in the place of honor at God's right hand in heaven." *Ephesians 1:19-20 TLB*

We have received a POWER to help us make all the changes that are necessary to be made in our lives. God doesn't give us directives and then not empower us to be able to change. He knows that we cannot make these changes in our own strength. He knows that our own will is not enough to change. So He has given us a POWER to change. This power that we've been given is called DUNAMIS! Dunamis is the power that comes from God! It is the power that He has supplied to help us to transform.

Over the next few days, we will look at different aspects of this Dunamis power so we can really understand the depth of His empowerment.

The first aspect of this power that we will examine is defined as 'a moral power and excellent soul.' This Dunamis has the ability to give us moral power for an excellent soul. Our soul consists of our mind, our will, and our emotions. Imagine that God endued us with power that will cause us to have an excellent operating soul – a soul that can potentially live free from such things as depression, oppression, fear, and worry. Well, that's exactly what this power possesses the ability to do. And guess what? It's on the inside of each of us. It comes to us through the gift of the Holy Spirit. This is exciting news for every Believer! We have the power to overcome every 'soulish' dysfunction. Nothing should have the power to overtake us. We should be the ones overthrowing dysfunction in our lives.

In our scripture text today, Paul prays that we would "begin to understand how incredibly great His power is to help those who believe in Him." Are you a believer? If you are, then His power, that Dunamis, is available to help you in every situation, including those that exist in your soul! It's time for you to stop accepting depression and fear and anxiety. It's time for you to wage war against it! You've been empowered by God to win this war! This is the place where the supernatural power of God that is in you rises up and begins to fight against everything foreign in your soul. Fear, anxiety, depression, even offense, are foreign to the soul of a believer. They don't match, nor do they work alongside, a born again spirit! Therefore, God has given the Believer this Dunamis to drive those things out of our lives once and for all!

Today, you can activate Dunamis power in your life with one simple prayer:

"Heavenly Father, as your child, I realize that according to Ephesians 1:19-20, You have given unto me the POWER, the DUNAMIS, to overcome everything that comes against my soul. I believe that power resides on the inside of me by virtue of the Holy Spirit Who resides on the inside of me. Today, I activate that power in my life, that supernatural ability given to me that causes me to have an EXCELLENT SOUL! Today, I use that Power to cast down spirits of depression, oppression, fear, anxiety, offense, doubt, despair, disappointment, bitterness, resentment, hopelessness, and any other thing that hinders me from walking in the liberty wherewith Christ has set me free! I declare myself WHOLE IN MY SOUL, IN JESUS' NAME! Amen!"

Reflections:

_____
_____
_____
_____
_____
_____
_____
_____
_____
_____
_____
_____
_____
_____
_____
_____
_____
_____
_____
_____
_____

Day 44

An Excellent Soul, Wow!

"I pray that you will begin to understand how incredibly great his power is to help those who believe him. It is that same mighty power that raised Christ from the dead and seated him in the place of honor at God's right hand in heaven." *Ephesians 1:19-20 TLB*

We talked yesterday about that Dunamis power giving us the ability to have an excellent soul. I want to continue today with more about having an excellent soul and what that means for us as believers. For a person to be in charge of their emotions instead of their emotions being in charge of them is a great feat! It will create the 'wow-factor' in your life! What does that mean? The ability to control your emotions will definitely increase the quality of your life.

We all know people whose emotions are out of control. Of course that's not us, no! But we know somebody, right? We may know, or may have been the victim of, someone who was emotionally abused. It is no fun. Perhaps, if we really admit it, there've been times that in our unhealed places, we may have reacted emotionally to a situation, and the outcome was not good. Some of us go into abusive relationships because we have no self-worth or self-confidence. We buy homes or cars to try to prove our significance to others. Many times we can't afford these purchases. They were made on a whim and out of a warped emotional state. Many people pay for years for choices they made while their emotions were out of whack. Some are in prison today, mentally, emotionally, and even physically, because they never mastered the art of controlling their soul, which includes their emotions.

How wonderful it would be if we would use that God-given power called Dunamis to be able to get our emotions in check. That Dunamis power will rise up in the midst of a crisis and cause you to make calm and rational decisions. It will allow you access to the wisdom of the Holy Spirit that will give you strategies when things aren't going right. When you learn how to rely on this power, you will find yourself operating at a superior level in your mind, your will, and your emotions! That creates a wow-factor for you. You will begin to see things that had been able to get you down, or make you angry or anxious, no longer have the ability to do so. It would appear as if you now have 'soul super powers' and you do! You have been endued with power from the Holy Spirit, and you have within your soul a supernatural ability to make right choices and sound decisions in every area of your life. You now have a supernatural ability from God to be strong in your mind and emotions even if depressing things happen to you and around you. The Power, the Dunamis, is available for you to live SUPERNATUALLY, WOW!

Take a few minutes today to examine your soul. Are there

areas in which you can honestly say that you are not emotionally sound? Maybe you've been hurt by someone or you may be experiencing feelings of depression over some disappointment or something. Write those areas down. Then pray, naming them one by one. Say something like, "Depression, I have been given the Dunamis power of God, and that power guarantees me an excellent soul. My emotions are part of my soul, and I command you now to come into upright order! I activate that Dunamis power in the area of my emotions now! I release all feelings of depression, and I receive the peace of God that passes all understanding."

Some would ask, "Is it that easy?" Well, everything is easier said than done. But as Believers, we must train our souls to come into alignment to the Kingdom of God and His Word! That happens with repetition. Doing this over and over, each time we face an attack on our souls. Remember you are the victor, not the victim! And this Dunamis power will create the Wow-Factor in your Life! Wow I'm free, Wow I'm Healed, Wow I'm living in peace!

Reflections:

_____
_____
_____
_____
_____
_____
_____
_____
_____
_____
_____
_____
_____
_____
_____
_____
_____
_____
_____
_____

Day 45

We Have the Power for Moral Excellence!

"For sin shall not [any longer] exert dominion over you, since you are not under Law [as slaves], but under grace [as subjects of God's favor and mercy]." *Romans 6:14 AMPC*

That same Dunamis power that gives us an excellent soul also gives us MORAL EXCELLENCE. That means sin and immorality don't have the right to reign in our lives. We've been empowered to overcome everything that would hinder our spiritual growth, no matter what it is. Many of us may no longer struggle with stealing or smoking or things like that. For that reason, we may think we're morally ok. But there are other things that, according to the 'moral standard' of the Kingdom of God, are not ok. For instance, there's this little thing called sarcasm, which I call 'Christian cussing.' Or, how about that bad attitude or the short way that you deal with people? How about being impatient or intolerant of people and their shortcomings? Our inability to deal with some of these areas presents a 'moral' breakdown in our lives. We are under a law from the Kingdom of Heaven to operate in Love. God has given us a way to do just that. Through His Dunamis power, we have the ability to overcome every moral mishap.

Our text today tells us that we no longer have to be under the dominion of sin because we are under God's grace. That Grace is God's empowerment in our lives, and that power includes His Dunamis! Sin doesn't have to dominate in our lives because we're empowered to overcome it. There's no such thing as 'I can't help it' or 'This thing always gets the better of me.' No! Those excuses don't hold water because we've been endued with supernatural power to overcome every moral sin. A moral sin doesn't necessarily have to be something big either; it can be any of the shortcomings we have in our lives. Lying is a moral sin. There's no such thing as a 'little white lie.' A lie is a lie! It is morally wrong in the Kingdom of God. You see, our Heavenly Father has empowered us to defeat every potentially weak area in our lives. He's given us this Dunamis that we can draw from and overcome the temptation to lie, or steal, or have a bad attitude, or to be sarcastic.

I don't know if you've heard of the new term 'hangry.' It means you're angry because you're hungry. Now this may be funny, and yes, it is a made-up term, but nonetheless, it is something that many people may experience. I'm using this example because we give many excuses for being rude, or out of control of our emotions. But in the Kingdom of God, there are no excuses. We are supposed to practice the law of kindness at all times. Relying on God's empowerment gives us the ability to do just that. We can be kind even when we're irritated or frustrated. We need to take a few minutes to pray, pray in the Spirit, and ask God to help us right in the very moment that we need Him. He will do it!

Then resist the temptation to be snappy or curt with someone. I've tried it and it works! Again, these exercises to manage our soul take time and consistency. But it can be done, and we have the power of God in us to aid us in getting it done.

Take a moment today to examine your attitude. Are you sarcastic, irritable, or frustrated? Do you find yourself blaming others for your behavior? Well, it's time to stop and take stock of your own emotions. Ask the Holy Spirit to show you those areas that are not submitted to the laws that govern His Kingdom. Then actively go about making sure that those areas come into alignment. It may not be as easy as it sounds, but it's also not as hard as we sometimes suppose it to be. You can do it! You have the Dunamis power of God on the inside of you!

Reflections:

_____
_____
_____
_____
_____
_____
_____
_____
_____
_____
_____
_____
_____
_____
_____
_____
_____
_____
_____
_____
_____

Day 46

We Have Strength (Dunamis Power) for All Things!

"I have strength for all things in Christ Who empowers me [I am ready for anything and equal to anything through Him Who infuses inner strength into me; I am self-sufficient in Christ's sufficiency]." *Philippians 4:13 AMPC*

I love this translation of Philippians 4:13, "I have strength for ALL things in Christ Who empowers me." Christ, the Anointing, empowers us to be able to go through all things. He empowers us to be able to face ALL things, to endure ALL things. There is nothing you can't do or overcome with this empowerment. The only reason the enemy gets the advantage in your life is because you don't realize that you've been empowered. The anointing in us empowers us to be overcomers! Stop letting the things of this world defeat you. Stop allowing bad attitudes and discouragement and anxiety to rule your life. You have the power to overcome it ALL!
Say this out loud, "There is nothing that the enemy can throw my way that can overtake me. I have power through Christ, the Anointing, to overcome ALL things." I don't

care if you have to say this a hundred times a day, keep confessing it until it manifests in your life. You have the power!

The scripture says, "I am ready for anything and equal to anything through Him Who INFUSES INNER STRENGTH into me." Just think, the Anointing is infusing you with an inner strength that is unequalled. That is why sometimes we see people go through things and wonder how they had the strength to make it through. It's that inner infusion that comes from the Anointing. There are some people who'll tap into that strength for certain situations, like sickness or disease, or to overcome a big challenge in their life, but will not tap into it to get their heart right or to defeat a spirit of offense. It's available for ALL things. No matter what it is that you may be up against, you're empowered and infused with inner strength by the Anointing to overcome!

Now don't confuse this with not having to go through something at all. We are infused with strength *because* we have to go through things. The Anointing simply assures our victory! Glory to God! Our victory is assured by reason of the Anointing!

We are self-sufficient, but not like the world sees self-sufficiency. We are self-sufficient through Christ's (the Anointing's) sufficiency. The Anointing makes us self-sufficient; that is, not having to rely on anything in this broken and insufficient realm that is falling apart day by day. Imagine your sufficiency being totally dependent upon Christ, the Anointed One and His anointing! How can you lose? You can't when you become self-sufficient in His sufficiency! Praise God!

Today, take a good look at your life. There may be some areas where you've been self-sufficient in your own sufficiency. Maybe you've taken on some frustrations or negativity that are part of the mindset of this realm. You had to do it in order to survive. But now that you're in Christ (the Anointing), you no longer have to depend on those things because you've been empowered and infused with inner strength from God and you can depend on Him to see you through!

As you reflect today, write down some areas in your life where you need that infusing to overcome some of your insufficiencies. Be honest, this is between you and God!

Reflections:

_____
_____
_____
_____
_____
_____
_____
_____
_____
_____
_____
_____
_____
_____
_____
_____
_____
_____
_____

Day 47

We Have Joint Seating With Christ

"And He raised us up together with Him and made us sit down together [giving us joint seating with Him] in the heavenly sphere [by virtue of our being] in Christ Jesus (the Messiah, the Anointed One]." *Ephesians 2:6 AMPC*

This is one of my favorite verses of scripture. Can you imagine that we are actually seated together with Christ in Heavenly Places? I always say, "Jesus is seated in Heaven for us and we are walking the earth for Him." We are in a partnership with Him. God has given Him full authority, and because we are seated with Him, we have full authority as well. In the Kingdom, being 'seated' is a sign of authority. You never see a King standing in front of His throne. No. He is always seated, because it denotes authority and dominion. Well, Ephesians is letting us know that we are now 'seated' in authority with Jesus. We have dominion in this earth because of our 'seat' in Heaven.

This is another reason why there is nothing in this realm that should be lording over you. Nothing should have dominion over you. You are a King. You're seated with Jesus in Heavenly Places. We're represented by Jesus in the Heavenly sphere. The things of this earth are subject to you just like they are subject to Jesus. That's why Luke 10:19 tells us, "Behold, I give unto you power to tread upon serpents and scorpions and over ALL the power of the enemy and NOTHING SHALL BY IN ANY MEANS HURT YOU!" Why can Jesus make such a bold statement? Because He knows where you're seated. He knows your level of authority in the earth, and He is trying to get you to know it too. All things are under our feet, ALL THINGS. There is nothing in this earth realm that is supposed to have dominion over us, not one thing! That is good news for every Believer – to know that we have full authority in this realm. The only authority that the devil has is the authority we give him. Now, if you've given the enemy any authority through your words, attitudes, or actions, you need to take it back. You need to close the door on all negativity and all fear. Close the door once and for all on oppressive thoughts and lies of the devil in your body, in your family, in your finances! You've been placed Higher than all of those things, and to allow them to overtake your life is to remove yourself from your 'seat.'

Sit back down! Yes, sit back down and take your rightful place of authority through the anointing of God, and put all things under your feet. He's given you authority (Dunamis power) over all the power of the enemy and NOTHING BY ANY MEANS SHALL HURT YOU! That's His promise to you and me. And what a powerful promise it is.

Today, I want you to meditate on this promise. Think about what it means to be a King sitting on a throne. Think about the authority that the King has and how everything must obey the King. Now imagine that YOU are that King and begin to speak to the things in your life that need to straighten up or get out! Don't play around with them. You have authority. You are the King of your life. Now take Dominion!

Reflections:

_____
_____
_____
_____
_____
_____
_____
_____
_____
_____
_____
_____
_____
_____
_____
_____
_____
_____
_____
_____

Day 48

Just How High Are We Seated?

"Which He exerted in Christ when He raised Him from the dead and seated Him at His [own] right hand in the heavenly [places], Far above all rule and authority and power and dominion and every name that is named [above every title that can be conferred], not only in this age *and* in this world, but also in the age *and* the world which are to come." *Ephesians 1:20-21 AMPC*

Our scripture text today tells us just how high we are really seated. It says that Jesus was seated at the right hand of the Father FAR ABOVE ALL, three of my favorite words, far…above…all! There is nothing in your life that even comes close to your 'seat.' NOTHNG! My pastor used to read it like this in his Guyanese dialect, "Faaaarrrrr above all…." He'd really put the emphasis on how far above everything in this earth Jesus' throne is. And guess what? If we're seated there with Him, then we are seated faaaarrrrr above all, as well. So you see, sickness and disease can't really do any harm to you. Poverty and brokenness should never have dominion in your life. Your seat is above all of these things. That's why for us to tolerate these things in our lives is to get up from our seat of authority and walk around like one who does not know his authority.

The scripture then begins to list the things that we are seated faaaarrrrr above: ALL RULE AND AUTHORITY AND POWER AND DOMINION that is in this earth realm or any realm below Heaven. It says EVERY NAME THAT IS NAMED. Cancer is a name that must bow to the Name of Jesus! Brokenness is a name that must bow to the Name of Jesus! Poverty is a name that must bow to the Name of Jesus! It says EVERY NAME. There isn't a name under heaven that is not subject to the authority of the Kingdom of Heaven. Once it has a name, it must bow!

The scripture continues, "and every title that can be conferred." Now that's a big one, because there are people with titles that may have made a decision about you, or your family, or your situation. Maybe a lawyer, or a doctor, or judge, maybe your boss, but ALL TITLES and their decisions regarding you, are subject to the authority of the Kingdom of Heaven. They are subject to your seat! Glory to God! That's why these lower entities of authority can never win over the Superior Authority of the Seat of the Anointing!

Today, as we are nearing the end of our 50-day journey, realize the authority that you possess. Realize that you are seated jointly with Jesus Christ and that you have access to the same power (Dunamis) that He has access to. Nothing in this realm, or under heaven, has a right to rule and dominate in your life unless you allow it.

Make this faith declaration:

"I will no longer allow anything that exists under heaven to dominate in my life! I am free from the control of every lower entity of power and authority. I take my spiritual position being seated together with Christ Jesus, faaaaarrrr above all principalities, powers, might, and dominion. I join myself to the Anointed One and His Anointing, and I walk in full assurance that I have the victory in every area of my life. In Jesus' Name, Amen!"

Reflections:

_____
_____
_____
_____
_____
_____
_____
_____
_____
_____
_____
_____
_____
_____
_____
_____
_____
_____
_____
_____
_____
_____
_____

Day 49

A Renewed Mind

"Do not be conformed to this world (this age), [fashioned after and adapted to its external, superficial customs], but be transformed (changed) by the [entire] renewal of your mind [by its new ideals and its new attitude], so that you may prove [for yourselves] what is the good and acceptable and perfect will of God, *even* the thing which is good and acceptable and perfect [in His sight for you]." *Romans 12:2 AMPC*

Well, we are almost at the end of this 50-day journey. I hope that you have been inspired to dismantle old and non-profitable mindsets and begin to reconstruct new ones. When the Lord gave us the instruction in Romans 12:2 to be transformed by the RENEWING OF OUR MINDS, He also equipped us to do so. He cannot and will not make a request of us that He has not designed us to be able to carry out. The point is that each of us must take 'on-purpose' steps every day to renew or reconstruct our paradigms. Every day we get brand new opportunities to renew our minds. Every day we are faced with decisions and choices that will help us to dismantle the old way of thinking and rebuild new systems of thought.

You probably have heard that after 21 days of doing something, it becomes a habit in your life. Well, it is my prayer that after these 50 days, the habit that has been formed is that you are now 'thinking about what you're thinking about.' That you no longer allow toxic thinking to take up room in your mind. I pray that you examine your thought life and that you make it a lifetime habit of purging old systems of thought and negative mindsets. Realize that these old mindsets will prevent you from completely carrying out the Will of God. The way that you will impact this world's system with your assignment is that you are able to carry it out to the fullest. This requires that you have the 'mind of Christ.' God does not want us to just *conform* to this world's way of thinking. He wants us to *impact* this world with *His* way of thinking.

With a Renewed Mind, we are able to tap into the Supernatural Realm of God. We are able to take the limits off in our minds and just believe that nothing shall be impossible for us through Him! We are limited when our mindsets are rooted in this natural realm. This realm will never allow us to think His thoughts or even believe that He wants the best for us. Therefore, it is a must that we make this transition. Our missions are depending on it. Remember that 'Creation is groaning, waiting for the manifestations of the Sons of God!' That's us, we're those Sons! It is time for some Kingdom manifestation in this earth Realm! We have some work to do, and we'd better get our minds right in order to carry out that work!

Keep arresting your stinking thinking. Don't let it run

rampant and hinder your assignment. Dismantle old mindsets and keep building new ones. Stay rooted and grounded in the Word of God. Our best, most miraculous, days are yet ahead of us!

Reflections:

Day 50

Take a Praise Break

"Hallelujah! Yes, praise the Lord! Praise him in his Temple and in the heavens he made with mighty power. Praise him for his mighty works. Praise his unequaled greatness. Praise him with the trumpet and with lute and harp. Praise him with the drums and dancing. Praise him with stringed instruments and horns. Praise him with the cymbals, yes, loud clanging cymbals. Let everything alive give praises to the Lord! *You* praise him! Hallelujah!" *Psalms 150 TLB*

Well, we have come to the end of this journey. I trust that these last 50 days have been a mind-renewing experience for you! I trust that you have taken the time to reflect on the ways that you have been thinking and have taken deliberate steps to transform your mind! Remember, you have the power (Dunamis), the grace, and the God-given ability to do it. Don't ever let the enemy trick you into thinking 'this is just the way I am.' NO! It's not just the way you are. You have the ability to change your mind and thereby change your LIFE!

You are your most precious commodity. You were created in the image and likeness of God. You are the vessel He has chosen to use in this earth. For this reason alone, you are worth every investment of time, money, and energy that you put into yourself to transform into what He needs you to be. I challenge you to use this book as a resource to consistently work on yourself, work on your mindset and perceptions. Remember, they guide your very life! Invest in yourself. Take time every day to think about what you're thinking about. Take time to uproot all toxic, non-productive, thought patterns. Dismantle old mental structures that were formed outside of the Word of God. They hinder you from moving forward. You take the responsibility for your own garden (mind) and the seeds that are planted there and are allowed to grow! Tend to your garden EVERY DAY! And above all, take the time each day to PRAISE THE LORD!

Our scripture text today commands us to PRAISE THE LORD! This is not just a suggestion. Nor is it just something that we are to do when we greet one another. No! It is something that we are commanded to do! Psalms 33:1 says, "Praise is comely for the upright." *Comely* is translated *beautiful, suitable, seemly*. It's something we ought to be doing on a regular basis. Our souls should be accustomed to giving our God praise!

Psalms 150 tells us to Praise Him wherever we go! Praise Him for the mighty works that He has done! God has done some great things for you. Take time today to think about the great things that He has done. Think about the small, intricate details of your life that He has taken care of. Think about how He has kept you and blessed you.

Praise Him for His unequalled greatness! There is none, absolutely no one, or nothing, GREATER than our GOD! No problem, no struggle, no person, no demon, no addiction, no sickness, no lack, NOTHING IS GREATER THAN OUR GOD! Your past is not greater, your failures are not greater, even your accomplishments are not greater than God! He deserves all our praise. Praise the Lord!

Praise Him with the instruments! Praise Him with your VOICE! Praise Him with your hands, praise Him with your dance! Let everything that LIVES and HAS BREATH, PRAISE THE LORD!

Reflections:

_____
_____
_____
_____
_____
_____
_____
_____
_____
_____
_____
_____
_____
_____
_____
_____
_____
_____

Appendix

Bible Translations

All Bible scriptures are King James Version, unless otherwise indicated. Used by the permission of Zondervan.

AMP	Amplified
AMPC	Amplified, Classic Edition
CEV	Contemporary English Version
ERV	Easy-to-Read Version
ESV	English Standard Version
GW	God's Word Translation
KJV	King James Version
MSG	The Message
NKJV	New King James Version
NLT	New Living Translation
TLB	The Living Bible

About the Author

Michelle Trotter is an Apostle and co-pastor of House of Jubilee Ministries, located in Euclid, Ohio, where she faithfully serves alongside her husband, Apostle Will Trotter. She is the founder of Michelle Trotter Ministries, the umbrella for her personal itinerate ministry, GRACE Women's Ministry, Kingdom Queens Mentoring Association (KQMA), and Leading Ladies Fellowship. The focus of Apostle Michelle's ministry is to help women become restored in their soul (mind, will, and emotions). Her mentoring program, KQMA, is geared toward maturing women of God and helping them take the next step into discovering their Kingdom Assignments. Leading Ladies Fellowship serves female pastors, co-pastors, and ministers in the Body of Christ. One of her favorite areas of ministry is the 'Mind Clinic' – a course she teaches that is geared toward helping the body of Christ learn the biblical and physiological dynamics of renewing the mind. All these ministries lend to the development and accountability of the Body of Christ.

Made in the USA
Lexington, KY
13 August 2019